SIMPLE
CAST IRON
COOKING

SIMPLE CAST IRON COOKING

13-Digit ISBN: 978-1-64643-319-3
10-Digit ISBN: 1-64643-319-X

This book may be ordered by mail from the publisher. Please include $5.99 for postage and handling.
Please support your local bookseller first!

Books published by Cider Mill Press Book Publishers are available at special discounts for bulk purchases in the United States by corporations, institutions, and other organizations. For more information, please contact the publisher.

Cider Mill Press Book Publishers
"Where good books are ready for press"
PO Box 454
12 Spring Street
Kennebunkport, Maine 04046

Visit us online!
cidermillpress.com

Typography: Acumin Pro, Dunbar Low

Image Credits: Pages 4, 23, 37, 39, 52–53, 57, 70–71, 74, 77, 80–81, 82, 86–87, 89, 90, 95, 96, 99, 102–103, 115, 117, 122, 125, 126, 130, 133, 141, 153, 154, 157, 158, 161, 172, 179, 187, 188, and 207 courtesy of Cider Mill Press. All other images used under official license from Shutterstock.com.

Printed in China

Front cover image: Pan-Seared Strip Steak, see page 185
Front endpaper image: Steak with Peppers & Onions, see page 113
Back endpaper image: Cherry Clafoutis, see page 217

1 2 3 4 5 6 7 8 9 0
First Edition

SIMPLE
CAST IRON
COOKING

OVER 100 FLAVORFUL RECIPES
THAT BRING NEW TASTES TO TRADITION

CIDER MILL PRESS

BOOK PUBLISHERS
KENNEBUNKPORT, MAINE

CONTENTS

INTRODUCTION

Simplicity is the polestar in the kitchen. Other things are important, of course—a feel for proper seasoning, patience, timing—but at the end of the day, the success of your preparations, and the smiles they produce, are largely dependent on your ability to remain straightforward. Not many offerings are better than a perfectly seared grass-fed steak seasoned with nothing more than salt and pepper, for instance, but to get this right one must resist the temptation to dress it up, and, even more important, to turn it before that browned crust has developed.

A large part of the beauty of cooking with cast iron is that it enforces this simplicity. Cast iron's ability to conduct heat and maintain it means that it is not the place to execute a delicate sauce or those byzantine preparations that dazzle the eye. Instead, one must always respect the ingredients placed upon cast iron, doing all you can to remain uncomplicated, using the unique abilities of this material to capture their essence.

Cast iron's versatility is another major piece of its appeal. It is as comfortable on the stovetop as it is in the oven or over a campfire, and the range of dishes a standard skillet can turn out—everything from an airy frittata and a hearty stew to a beautifully burnished loaf of bread, it's fair to wonder how kitchen supply stores convince people to purchase the specialized wares that crowd the shelves. Somehow, it is not outlandish to claim that one could not have another piece of cookware in the house other than a cast-iron skillet and still manage splendidly in the kitchen. In fact, if you're a person that loves to cook but despises the sink full of dishes that tend to result, you may well want to go this route.

That generous nature is dependent on a little TLC from you, however, as a cast-iron cookware is only as good as its level of seasoning. This coating of polymerized oil allows cast iron to remain nonstick and prevents it from rusting. It is not difficult to maintain a proper level of seasoning, but it does require some devotion and consistency after the cookware has been used. First off, many devotees claim that soap should never touch a piece of cast iron. In truth, if your seasoning is on point, a little bit of soap is OK to use in particularly gritty preparations. But for the most part, a little bit of water and a sponge or a brush with plastic bristles will suffice to clean off the cookware. Once that step has been accomplished, cast iron needs to be thoroughly dried and rubbed with a little bit of canola, avocado, or vegetable oil to ensure it remains in good condition.

With that, and this book in hand, you're ready to become a cast-iron connoisseur. You'll notice, as you flip through the pages, that the preparations have been plucked from cuisines all across the globe. That cosmopolitan quality is inherent in cast-iron's very construction—it is used prominently by cooks everywhere, and has been for centuries. Sure, this widespread following is tied to its sturdiness and versatility. But it is also a testament to cast iron's simple, pleasing aesthetics.

Cast iron is the choice for those who cherish the timeless, the beautifully crafted, and the simple. In other words, each and every one of us.

BREAKFAST
& BREADS

In the morning, few things are simpler than grabbing a cup of coffee and a piece of fruit and running out the door. But there are times where we want—need, really—to take a few minutes and make something worth lingering over. This chapter will provide in these moments, freighting the breakfast table with plenty of deliciousness.

And, in those instances where you can't laze through the morning, is there anything quite like a slice of homemade bread slathered in good butter? In truth, no. Fortunately, breads are yet another area where cast iron proves up to the challenge. Whether it be a skillet cornbread or a painstakingly developed loaf of sourdough, your baking will reach new heights thanks to this wondrous material.

FRENCH TOAST

INGREDIENTS

6 large eggs

½ cup half-and-half

2 tablespoons sugar

1 teaspoon kosher salt

½ teaspoon pure vanilla extract

1 teaspoon triple sec

1 tablespoon honey, plus more
for serving

1 teaspoon orange zest

1 loaf of brioche or challah, cut
into thick slices

4 to 6 tablespoons unsalted
butter

Confectioners' sugar, for dusting

Fresh berries, for serving

DIRECTIONS

1 Preheat the oven to 200°F. Whisk together the eggs, half-and-half,
sugar, salt, vanilla extract, triple sec, honey, and orange zest.

2 Place the slices of bread in a single layer in a baking dish and pour
the egg mixture over the top. Let the bread soak for 3 minutes, turn
the slices over, and soak for 2 to 3 minutes.

3 Place some of the butter in a large cast-iron skillet and melt it
over medium-high heat. Working in batches to avoid crowding the
pan, add the bread and cook until brown and crispy on both sides,
about 5 minutes. Place the cooked French toast on a plate and
place it in the oven. Add more butter to the pan when it starts to
look dry.

4 When all of the French toast is cooked, dust each portion with
confectioners' sugar and serve with berries and additional honey.

YIELD: 4 SERVINGS
ACTIVE TIME: 30 MINUTES
TOTAL TIME: 40 MINUTES

CHILAQUILES

INGREDIENTS

½ lb. tomatillos, husks removed, rinsed well

2 garlic cloves

½ red onion, sliced thin

2 guajillo chile peppers, stems and seeds removed

2 dried chiles de arbol, stems and seeds removed

2 cups canola oil

2 tablespoons extra-virgin olive oil

1 lb. corn tortillas, cut into 40 triangles

Salt, to taste

4 large eggs

2 cups shredded queso fresco, plus more for serving

Fresh cilantro, chopped, for garnish

Sour cream, for serving

Lime wedges, for serving

DIRECTIONS

1 Bring water to a boil in a medium saucepan. Add the tomatillos, garlic, and half of the onion and cook until tender, about 7 minutes.

2 While the vegetables are boiling, place the chiles in a bowl and pour some hot water over them. Let the chiles soak for 15 minutes.

3 Drain the vegetables, place them in a blender, and puree until smooth. Leave the puree in the blender.

4 Place the canola oil in a large, deep cast-iron skillet and warm it to 350°F. Add the tortillas and fry until crispy, about 3 minutes. Place the fried tortillas on a paper towel–lined plate and let them drain. Wipe out the skillet.

5 Preheat the oven to 350°F. Add the chiles to the puree in the blender and puree until smooth. Season the puree generously with salt and set it aside.

6 Place the olive oil in the skillet and warm it over medium heat. Add the remaining onion and cook, stirring occasionally, until translucent, about 3 minutes.

7 Add the puree and the tortillas to the skillet and stir until everything is combined. Crack the eggs on top, crumble the queso fresco over everything, and place the skillet in the oven.

8 Bake until the egg whites are set and the cheese is slightly melted. Remove the skillet from the oven and garnish the chilaquiles with cilantro. Serve with sour cream, additional queso fresco, and lime wedges.

YIELD: 6 SERVINGS
ACTIVE TIME: 15 MINUTES
TOTAL TIME: 1 HOUR AND 10 MINUTES

BAKED EGG CASSEROLE

INGREDIENTS

12 large eggs

½ cup half-and-half

3 plum tomatoes, sliced

1 cup chopped spinach

½ cup chopped scallions

1 cup freshly grated Parmesan cheese, plus more for garnish

1 tablespoon fresh thyme

1 tablespoon unsalted butter

Salt and pepper, to taste

DIRECTIONS

1   Preheat the oven to 350°F. In a mixing bowl, combine the eggs, ¼ cup water, and half-and-half.

2   Place all of the other ingredients, except for the butter, salt, and pepper, in the mixing bowl and whisk to combine.

3   Coat a medium cast-iron skillet with the butter and then pour the mixture into the skillet.

4   Season the egg mixture with salt and pepper, place the skillet in the oven, and bake until the eggs are set in the center, about 45 minutes.

5   Remove the pan from the oven and let the casserole stand for 10 minutes before serving. Sprinkle additional Parmesan over the casserole and enjoy.

YIELD: 4 SERVINGS

ACTIVE TIME: 15 MINUTES

TOTAL TIME: 1 HOUR

ZUCCHINI & HERB FRITTATA

INGREDIENTS

4 cups shredded zucchini

Salt and pepper, to taste

2 tablespoons extra-virgin olive oil

6 scallions, trimmed and sliced thin

2 garlic cloves, minced

4 eggs

⅓ cup milk

1 cup crumbled feta cheese

2 tablespoons chopped fresh dill

1 tablespoon chopped fresh oregano

1 tablespoon chopped fresh parsley

DIRECTIONS

1 Preheat the oven to 350°F. Place the zucchini in a colander, season it generously with salt, and toss to coat. Let the zucchini drain for 20 minutes.

2 Place the zucchini in a linen towel and wring the towel to remove as much liquid as possible from the zucchini.

3 Place the olive oil in a medium cast-iron skillet and warm it over medium heat. Add the scallions and garlic and cook, stirring continually, for 1 minute. Add the zucchini and cook, stirring occasionally, until the moisture it releases has evaporated, 5 to 8 minutes. Remove the pan from heat and let the mixture cool.

4 Place the eggs and milk in a bowl and whisk until combined. Stir in the zucchini mixture, feta, and fresh herbs.

5 Pour the egg mixture into the cast-iron skillet, shaking the pan slightly to ensure it gets distributed evenly.

6 Place the frittata in the oven and bake until the center feels springy and the top is golden brown, about 25 minutes. Remove the frittata from the oven and let it rest for 5 minutes before enjoying.

YIELD: 4 SERVINGS
ACTIVE TIME: 25 MINUTES
TOTAL TIME: 1 HOUR

BLUEBERRY PANCAKES

INGREDIENTS

2 cups all-purpose flour

3 tablespoons sugar

1½ teaspoons baking powder

1½ teaspoons baking soda

1¼ teaspoons kosher salt

2½ cups buttermilk

2 large eggs

3 tablespoons unsalted butter, melted

1½ cups blueberries

Canola oil, as needed

DIRECTIONS

1 Preheat the oven to 250°F. Place a wire rack in a rimmed baking sheet and set it aside. Place the flour, sugar, baking powder, baking soda, and salt in a mixing bowl and whisk to combine. Make a well in the center of the mixture and pour the buttermilk into the well. Crack the eggs into the well and then add the melted butter.

2 Working from the center to the outer edge, incorporate the dry mixture and the wet mixture until it just comes together as a batter, taking care to not overwork the mixture. Add the blueberries and fold to incorporate. Let the batter rest at room temperature for 30 minutes.

3 Warm a large cast-iron skillet over low heat for 3 to 4 minutes. Coat the bottom of the skillet with canola oil, raise the heat to medium-low, and ladle ¼-cup portions of the batter into the skillet.

4 Cook the pancakes until the bottom sides are browned and bubbles start to appear on the surface, 2 to 3 minutes. Flip the pancakes over and cook until the other sides are golden brown, 1 to 2 minutes.

5 Transfer the cooked pancakes to the wire rack and place the baking sheet in the oven to keep them warm.

6 Repeat with the remaining batter, adding more canola oil to the pan when it starts to look dry.

BLUEBERRY PANCAKES, SEE PAGE 17

YIELD: 4 SERVINGS

ACTIVE TIME: 20 MINUTES

TOTAL TIME: 1 HOUR

SPINACH STRATA

INGREDIENTS

7 eggs, beaten

2 cups whole milk

1 cup shredded Swiss cheese

Pinch of freshly grated nutmeg

3 cups day-old bread pieces

2 teaspoons extra-virgin olive oil

1 yellow onion, minced

5 oz. baby spinach

Salt and pepper, to taste

DIRECTIONS

1   Preheat the oven to 400°F. Place the eggs and milk in a large mixing bowl and whisk to combine. Add the cheese and nutmeg and stir to incorporate. Add the bread pieces and let the mixture sit for 10 minutes.

2   Place the olive oil in a 10-inch cast-iron skillet and warm it over medium heat. Add the onion and spinach and cook, stirring occasionally, until the spinach has wilted and the onion is translucent, about 3 minutes. Remove the pan from heat.

3   Pour the egg mixture into the skillet and gently shake the pan to make sure the eggs are evenly distributed. Season the strata with salt and pepper.

4   Place the skillet in the oven and bake the strata until it is golden brown and springy in the center, about 25 minutes.

5   Remove the strata from the oven and let it cool for 10 minutes before enjoying.

YIELD: 8 SERVINGS

ACTIVE TIME: 30 MINUTES

TOTAL TIME: 2 HOURS AND 30 MINUTES

BUTTERNUT SQUASH QUICHE

INGREDIENTS

8 eggs

1 cup heavy cream

1 teaspoon kosher salt

¼ teaspoon black pepper

1 tablespoon extra-virgin olive oil

2 cups diced butternut squash (½-inch dice)

2 garlic cloves, minced

1 cup fresh spinach

1 teaspoon minced fresh rosemary

½ cup crumbled goat cheese

1 Perfect Piecrust (see page 192), blind baked in a 9-inch cast-iron skillet

DIRECTIONS

1   Preheat the oven to 350°F. Place the eggs, heavy cream, salt, and pepper in a mixing bowl and whisk until combined. Set the mixture aside.

2   Place the olive oil in a large cast-iron skillet and warm it over medium-high heat. Working in batches if necessary to avoid crowding the pan, add the butternut squash and cook, stirring occasionally, until it is nearly cooked through, about 10 minutes.

3   Add the garlic, spinach, and rosemary to the pan and cook, stirring frequently, until the spinach has wilted, about 2 minutes. Remove the pan from heat and let the vegetable mixture cool.

4   Sprinkle the goat cheese over the bottom of the baked crust and evenly distribute the vegetable mixture over the top. Pour the egg mixture into the crust, stopping when it reaches the top.

5   Place the quiche in the oven and bake until the center is set and the filling is lightly golden brown, 35 to 45 minutes.

6   Remove the quiche from the oven, transfer it to a cooling rack, and let it cool for 1 hour. The quiche will be enjoyable warm, at room temperature, or cold.

YIELD: 4 SERVINGS
ACTIVE TIME: 20 MINUTES
TOTAL TIME: 20 MINUTES

HUEVOS RANCHEROS

INGREDIENTS

1 (14 oz.) can of black beans, drained and rinsed

¾ cup extra-virgin olive oil

4 corn tortillas

3 large tomatoes

¼ onion

2 serrano chile peppers, stems and seeds removed, sliced

Salt, to taste

4 eggs

½ lb. queso fresco, shredded, for garnish

½ cup chopped fresh cilantro, for garnish

DIRECTIONS

1   Place the black beans in a small saucepan and bring them to a gentle simmer over medium heat. Reduce the heat to low and let the beans simmer.

2   Place half of the olive oil in a large cast-iron skillet and warm it over medium-high heat. Add the tortillas and fry for about 1 minute on each side. Transfer the tortillas to a paper towel–lined plate and let them drain.

3   Place the tomatoes, onion, and chiles in a blender and puree until smooth.

4   Place 2 tablespoons of the remaining olive oil in a small cast-iron skillet and warm over medium heat. Carefully add the puree, reduce the heat to low, and cook the salsa for 5 minutes. Season with salt and then set the salsa aside.

5   Place the remaining olive oil in the large cast-iron skillet, add the eggs, season the yolks generously with salt, and cook as desired.

6   To assemble, place an egg on a fried tortilla, spoon the salsa and black beans over the top, and garnish with the cheese and cilantro.

YIELD: 8 MUFFINS
ACTIVE TIME: 30 MINUTES
TOTAL TIME: 3 HOURS

ENGLISH MUFFINS

INGREDIENTS

7 oz. water

1 teaspoon active dry yeast

4½ teaspoons unsalted butter, softened

1 tablespoon sugar

1 egg

2 cups bread flour, plus more as needed

1 teaspoon kosher salt

Semolina flour, as needed

DIRECTIONS

1   Place the water and yeast in the work bowl of a stand mixer fitted with the dough hook, gently stir to combine, and let the mixture sit until it starts to foam, about 10 minutes.

2   Add the butter, sugar, egg, bread flour, and salt and knead on low for 1 minute. Raise the speed to medium and knead the mixture until it comes together as a smooth dough and begins to pull away from the side of the work bowl, about 5 minutes.

3   Coat a mixing bowl with nonstick cooking spray. Remove the dough from the work bowl, place it on a flour-dusted work surface, and shape it into a ball. Place the dough in the bowl, cover the bowl with plastic wrap, place it in a naturally warm spot, and let the dough rise until it has doubled in size.

4   Line an 18 x 13–inch baking sheet with parchment paper.

5   Place the dough on a flour-dusted work surface and divide it into eight pieces. Flatten each piece into a 3½-inch circle and place the circles on the baking sheet. Cover the muffins with plastic wrap, place them in a naturally warm spot, and let them rest for 30 minutes.

6   Preheat the oven to 350°F. Warm a large cast-iron skillet over low heat and lightly sprinkle the semolina flour over the pan. Working in batches of two or three at a time, place the muffins in the pan and cook until they are golden brown on both sides, 12 to 20 minutes. The internal temperature of the muffins should be 190°F. If the muffins browned too quickly and are not cooked through in the center, bake them in the oven for 5 to 10 minutes.

7   Let the muffins cool before slicing and enjoying.

ENGLISH MUFFINS, SEE PAGE 25

CINNAMON BUNS

DIRECTIONS

1 To prepare the filling, place all of the ingredients in the work bowl of a stand mixer fitted with a paddle attachment and beat on medium until the mixture is light and fluffy. Transfer to a mixing bowl and set it aside. Wipe out the work bowl of the stand mixer.

2 To prepare the glaze, place all of the ingredients in a mixing bowl and whisk to combine. Cover the bowl with plastic wrap and set the glaze aside.

3 To begin preparations for the dough, place the water and yeast in the work bowl of the stand mixer, gently stir, and let the mixture sit until it is foamy, about 10 minutes.

4 Add the eggs, oil, flour, sugar, and salt to the work bowl, fit the mixer with the dough hook, and work the mixture on low until the dough starts to come together, about 2 minutes. Raise the speed to medium and knead until the dough is elastic and pulls away from the side of the work bowl. Cover the bowl with plastic wrap, place it in a naturally warm spot, and allow the dough to rise until it has doubled in size, about 1 hour.

5 Turn the dough out onto a flour-dusted work surface. Use a rolling pin to roll the dough into a rectangle that is about 24 x 12 inches. Spread the filling evenly across the dough, leaving an inch of dough uncovered on the wide side closest to yourself. Sprinkle sugar lightly over the filling. This will help provide friction and allow for a tight roll.

6 Take the side farthest away and roll the dough into a tight spiral. Pinch the seam to seal the roll closed. Cut the roll into twelve 2-inch-wide buns.

7 Coat a large cast-iron skillet with nonstick cooking spray. Place the 12 buns in the pan in an even layer. Cover the buns with plastic wrap, place them in a naturally warm spot, and let them rise until doubled in size.

8 Preheat the oven to 350°F.

9 Remove the plastic wrap, place the skillet in the oven, and bake the buns until their internal temperature is 210°F, 20 to 30 minutes. Remove the buns from the oven and pour the glaze over them. Let them cool slightly before enjoying.

INGREDIENTS

For the Filling

1 cup unsalted butter, softened

1 cup sugar, plus more to taste

1 cup dark brown sugar

1 teaspoon pure vanilla extract

2 tablespoons cinnamon

For the Glaze

4 cups confectioners' sugar

½ cup water

1 teaspoon pure vanilla extract

Pinch of kosher salt

For the Dough

1½ cups lukewarm water (90°F)

1 tablespoon plus 2 teaspoons
active dry yeast

3 eggs

¼ cup extra-virgin olive oil

2 lbs. bread flour, plus more
as needed

¼ cup sugar, plus more
for dusting

1½ tablespoons kosher salt

YIELD: 4 TO 6 SERVINGS
ACTIVE TIME: 20 MINUTES
TOTAL TIME: 35 MINUTES

CHEESY HASH BROWNS

INGREDIENTS

4 large russet potatoes, peeled and shredded

4 tablespoons unsalted butter

1 teaspoon kosher salt

Black pepper, to taste

6 eggs

½ cup milk

1 cup shredded cheddar cheese

DIRECTIONS

1   Preheat the oven to 375°F. Place the potatoes in a linen towel and wring it to remove as much moisture from the potatoes as possible. Place the potatoes in a bowl.

2   Place the butter in a large cast-iron skillet and melt it over medium-high heat. Add the potatoes and salt and season with pepper. Press down on the potatoes to pack them into an even layer. Cook the potatoes, without stirring, for 5 minutes.

3   In a mixing bowl, whisk the eggs and milk until combined. Pour the mixture over the potatoes and shake the pan to help the egg mixture penetrate to the bottom. Sprinkle the cheese on top and then transfer the skillet to the oven.

4   Bake until the eggs are just set and the cheese is melted, about 10 minutes. Remove the skillet from the oven and enjoy.

SOURDOUGH STARTER

INGREDIENTS

1 cup water, at room temperature, plus more daily

2 cups all-purpose flour, plus more daily

DIRECTIONS

1   Place the water and flour in a large jar (the jar should be at least 1 quart). Combine the ingredients by hand, cover the jar, and let it stand in a sunny spot at room temperature for 24 hours.

2   Place 1 cup of the starter in a bowl, add 1 cup water and 2 cups all-purpose flour, and stir until thoroughly combined. Discard the remainder of the starter. Place the new mixture back in the jar and let it sit at room temperature for 24 hours. Repeat this process every day until you notice bubbles forming on the surface of the starter. This should take approximately 2 weeks. If it does not start to bubble after 2 weeks, feed it twice a day until it does.

3   Once the starter begins to bubble, it can be used in recipes. The starter can be stored at room temperature or in the refrigerator. If the starter is kept at room temperature, it must be fed once a day; if the starter is refrigerated, it can be fed every 3 to 6 days. The starter can be frozen for up to a month without feeding.

4   To feed the starter, place 1 cup of the starter in a bowl, add 1 cup flour and 1 cup water, and work the mixture with your hands until combined. Discard the remainder of the starter. It is recommended that you feed the starter 6 to 8 hours before making bread.

YIELD: 1 LARGE LOAF
ACTIVE TIME: 20 MINUTES
TOTAL TIME: 30 HOURS

SOURDOUGH BREAD

DIRECTIONS

1   Combine the 1⅔ cups water and the flour in a bowl and work the mixture until it just comes together as a dough. Cover the dough with plastic wrap and let it rest for 30 minutes.

2   Add the Sourdough Starter, salt, and remaining water to the dough. Knead for 10 minutes, until the dough is smooth and elastic. Place the dough in a bowl, cover with plastic wrap, and store in a naturally warm place for 4 hours.

3   Place the dough on a flour-dusted work surface and fold the left side of the dough to the right, fold the right side of the dough to the left, and fold the bottom toward the top. Form the dough into a rough ball, return it to the bowl, cover with plastic wrap, and let the dough rest for 30 minutes.

4   After 30 minutes, place the ball of dough on a flour-dusted work surface and repeat the folds made in Step 3. Form the dough into a ball, dust it with flour, and place it in a bowl with the seam facing up. Dust a linen towel with flour, cover the bowl with it, and place the bowl in the refrigerator overnight.

5   Approximately 2 hours before you are ready to bake the bread, remove it from the refrigerator, place it on a square of parchment paper, and let the bread come to room temperature.

6   Preheat the oven to 500°F. Place a covered cast-iron Dutch oven in the oven as it warms.

7   When the dough is at room temperature and the oven is ready, remove the Dutch oven from the oven and carefully lower the square of parchment paper with the ball of dough on it into the Dutch oven. Score the top of the dough with a very sharp knife or razor blade, making a long cut across the middle. Cover the Dutch oven, place it in the oven, and bake for 25 minutes.

8   Remove the lid from the Dutch oven, lower the oven's temperature to 480°F, and bake the bread until it is golden brown and sounds hollow when tapped, about 25 minutes.

9   Remove the bread from the oven and let it cool on a wire rack for 2 hours before slicing.

INGREDIENTS

1⅔ cups plus 1 teaspoon filtered water (78°F)

5 cups bread flour, plus more as needed

¾ cup Sourdough Starter (see page 33)

1½ teaspoons fine sea salt

YIELD: 1 LOAF

ACTIVE TIME: 30 MINUTES

TOTAL TIME: 21 HOURS

RUSTIC WHITE BREAD

DIRECTIONS

1 Place the flour and water in a large mixing bowl and work the mixture until it just comes together as a dough. Cover the bowl with a linen towel and let the mixture sit at room temperature for 45 minutes to 1 hour.

2 Sprinkle the yeast and salt over the dough and fold to incorporate them. Cover the bowl with the linen towel and let it stand for 30 minutes. Remove the towel, fold a corner of the dough to the center, and cover the dough. Repeat every 30 minutes until all of the corners have been folded in toward the center.

3 After the last fold, cover the dough with the linen towel and let it rest at room temperature for 12 hours.

4 Dust a work surface with flour and place the dough on it. Fold each corner of the dough to the center, flip the dough over, and roll it into a smooth ball. Dust your hands with flour as needed. Be careful not to press down on the dough too hard, as this will deflate it, preventing it from expanding properly in the oven. Dust a bowl with flour and place the dough, seam side down, in the bowl. Let it rest at room temperature until it has doubled in size, about 1 hour.

5 Preheat the oven to 475°F and place a covered cast-iron Dutch oven in the oven as it warms.

6 Turn the dough onto a flour-dusted work surface. Use a razor or a very sharp knife to score one side of the loaf and then place it, scored side up, on a square of parchment paper. Using oven mitts, carefully remove the Dutch oven from the oven. Carefully lower the square of parchment paper with the ball of dough on it into the Dutch oven. Cover the Dutch oven, place it in the oven, and bake the bread for 20 minutes.

7 Remove the lid from the Dutch oven and bake the loaf until it is golden brown and sounds hollow when tapped, 20 to 25 minutes.

8 Remove the bread from the oven and let it cool on a wire rack before slicing.

INGREDIENTS

4½ cups all-purpose flour, plus more as needed

1½ cups water (90°F)

¼ teaspoon (scant) active dry yeast

2¼ teaspoons fine sea salt

RUSTIC WHOLE WHEAT BREAD

DIRECTIONS

1   Place the flours and water in a large mixing bowl and work the mixture until it comes together as a dough. Cover the bowl with a linen towel and let the dough rest at room temperature for 45 minutes to 1 hour.

2   Sprinkle the yeast and salt over the dough and fold to incorporate them. Cover the bowl with the linen towel and let it rest at room temperature for 30 minutes.

3   Remove the towel, fold a corner of the dough into the center, and cover. Repeat every 30 minutes until all of the corners have been folded in toward the center. After the last fold, cover the dough with the linen towel and let it rest at room temperature for 12 hours.

4   Dust a work surface with flour and place the dough on it. Fold each corner of the dough into the center, turn the dough over, and roll it into a smooth ball. Dust your hands with flour as needed during this process. Be careful not to press down too hard on the dough, as this will deflate the dough, preventing it from expanding properly. Dust a bowl with flour and place the dough, seam side down, in the bowl. Let it rest at room temperature until it has roughly doubled in size, about 1 hour.

5   Preheat the oven to 475°F and place a covered cast-iron Dutch oven in the oven as it warms.

6   Turn the dough onto a flour-dusted work surface. Use a razor or a very sharp knife to score one side of the loaf and then place it, scored side up, on a square of parchment paper. Using oven mitts, carefully remove the Dutch oven from the oven. Carefully lower the square of parchment paper with the ball of dough on it into the Dutch oven. Cover the Dutch oven, place it in the oven, and bake the bread for 20 minutes.

7   Remove the lid from the Dutch oven and bake the loaf until it is golden brown and sounds hollow when tapped, 20 to 25 minutes.

8   Remove the bread from the oven and let it cool on a wire rack before slicing.

INGREDIENTS

3¼ cups all-purpose flour, plus more as needed

1¼ cups whole wheat flour

1½ cups water (90°F)

¼ teaspoon (scant) active dry yeast

2¼ teaspoons fine sea salt

YIELD: 12 SERVINGS

ACTIVE TIME: 20 MINUTES

TOTAL TIME: 1 HOUR

CORNBREAD

INGREDIENTS

½ cup honey

1½ cups unsalted butter, softened

3 cups plus 3¾ tablespoons all-purpose flour

½ lb. cornmeal

1 tablespoon plus 1 teaspoon baking powder

1 tablespoon kosher salt

1 cup sugar

4 eggs

2 cups milk

DIRECTIONS

1 Preheat the oven to 350°F. Coat a large cast-iron skillet with nonstick cooking spray.

2 Place the honey and one-third of the butter in a small saucepan and warm the mixture over medium heat until the butter has melted. Whisk to combine and set the mixture aside.

3 Place the flour, cornmeal, baking powder, and salt in a mixing bowl and whisk to combine. Set the mixture aside.

4 In the work bowl of a stand mixer fitted with the paddle attachment, cream the remaining butter and the sugar on medium until light and fluffy, about 5 minutes. Add the eggs and beat until incorporated. Add the dry mixture, reduce the speed to low, and beat until the mixture comes together as a smooth batter. Gradually add the milk and beat until incorporated.

5 Pour the batter into the skillet and gently tap it on a counter to remove any air bubbles and evenly distribute the batter. Place the pan in the oven and bake until a cake tester inserted into the center of the cornbread comes out clean, 25 to 30 minutes.

6 Remove the pan from the oven and place it on a wire rack. Brush the cornbread with the honey butter and serve it warm.

BISCUITS

INGREDIENTS

2 cups plus ½ cup buttermilk

¼ cup honey

5 cups plus 3¾ tablespoons all-purpose flour, plus more as needed

1 tablespoon kosher salt

3 tablespoons baking powder

1 cup unsalted butter, chilled and cubed; plus ¼ cup, melted

DIRECTIONS

1 Preheat the oven to 425°F. Coat a large cast-iron skillet with nonstick cooking spray. Place 2 cups of the buttermilk and the honey in a measuring cup and whisk to combine. Set the mixture aside.

2 Place the flour, salt, baking powder, and chilled butter in the work bowl of a stand mixer fitted with the paddle attachment and beat the mixture until combined and the butter has been reduced to pea-sized pieces, 5 to 10 minutes. Gradually add the buttermilk mixture and beat the mixture until it comes together as a slightly crumbly dough.

3 Transfer the dough to a flour-dusted work surface. Generously dust your hands and a roller with flour and then roll the dough into a ¾-inch-thick rectangle. Using a bench scraper, cut the dough into thirds and stack them on top of each other. Roll the dough out once more into a ¾-inch-thick rectangle.

4 Cut the dough into twelve 3-inch circles and arrange them side by side in the skillet. Brush the tops of the biscuits with the remaining buttermilk.

5 Place the pan in the oven and bake the biscuits until they are golden brown, 15 to 17 minutes.

6 Remove from the oven and place the biscuits on a wire rack to cool slightly. Brush them with the melted butter and enjoy warm.

SNACKS & SIDES

As those who are fanatical about fried food can attest, attaining that idealized crispy, golden brown exterior can prove difficult at home. These disappointments are due to the difficulty of keeping whatever fat one is cooking in hot enough once the preparation is added. Fortunately, cast iron eliminates this issue entirely, as its ability to conduct heat ensures that you achieve the longed-for result. And, should you desire something a little less rich, there's plenty of other options to nosh upon.

Many of these snacks can also work as sides, but, at some point, one must take a step back and attempt to bring some balance to their diet in the form of vegetables. Fortunately, cast iron shines here as well, able to supply the bit of char produce like eggplant, Brussels sprouts, and asparagus craves, as well as the leisurely braise in the oven that delicate veggies such as leeks benefit from.

YIELD: 4 SERVINGS

ACTIVE TIME: 25 MINUTES

TOTAL TIME: 1 HOUR AND 30 MINUTES

POPCORN CHICKEN

INGREDIENTS

3 garlic cloves, smashed

1 egg white

1 tablespoon soy sauce

1½ tablespoons sesame oil

½ teaspoon white pepper

1 tablespoon cornstarch

Salt, to taste

1 lb. boneless, skin-on chicken breast, cut into bite-size pieces

7 tablespoons tapioca starch, plus more as needed

2 cups canola oil

DIRECTIONS

1   Place the garlic, egg white, soy sauce, sesame oil, white pepper, cornstarch, and salt in a mixing bowl and stir to combine. Add the chicken, toss to coat, and cover the bowl. Chill in the refrigerator for 1 hour.

2   Dust a sheet pan with the tapioca starch, add the chicken, and turn it in the starch until it is coated, adding more tapioca starch as necessary.

3   Place the canola oil in a cast-iron Dutch oven and warm it to 350°F over medium heat. Shake the chicken to remove any excess tapioca starch. Working in batches to avoid overcrowding the Dutch oven, carefully add the chicken to the pot, and fry until golden brown and cooked through, 8 to 10 minutes.

4   Transfer the cooked chicken to a paper towel–lined plate to drain and briefly let it cool before serving.

YIELD: 6 SERVINGS

ACTIVE TIME: 40 MINUTES

TOTAL TIME: 1 HOUR AND 15 MINUTES

SCALLION PANCAKES

DIRECTIONS

1 Place the flour and water in a mixing bowl and work the mixture until it comes together as a shaggy dough. Transfer the dough to a flour-dusted work surface and knead it until it is a tacky, nearly smooth ball. Cover the dough with plastic wrap and let it rest for 30 minutes.

2 Place 1 tablespoon of the canola oil, the sesame oil, and 1 tablespoon of flour in a small bowl and stir to combine. Set the mixture aside.

3 Divide the dough in half, cover one piece with plastic wrap, and set it aside. Place the other piece on a flour-dusted work surface and roll it into a 12-inch circle. Drizzle approximately 1 tablespoon of the oil-and-flour mixture over the round and use a pastry brush to spread the mixture evenly. Sprinkle half of the salt and scallions over the round and roll it into a cylinder. Coil the cylinder into a spiral and flatten it with your palm. Cover with plastic wrap and repeat with the other piece of dough.

4 Warm a large cast-iron skillet over low heat. Roll one piece of dough into a 9-inch round and make a slit, approximately ½ inch deep, in the center of the round, making sure not to cut all the way through. Cover the round with plastic wrap and repeat with the other piece of dough.

5 Coat the bottom of the skillet with some of the remaining canola oil and raise the heat to medium-low. Place 1 round in the pan, cover it, and cook until the pancake is golden brown, about 1 minute. Drizzle a little canola oil over the pancake, use a pastry brush to spread it evenly, and carefully flip the pancake over. Cover the pan and cook until browned on that side, about 1 minute.

6 Remove the cover and cook the pancake until it is crisp and a deep golden brown, about 30 seconds. Flip the pancake over and cook until crispy on that side, another 30 seconds. Remove from the pan, transfer to a wire rack to cool, and cook the other pancake. When both pancakes have been cooked, slice each one into wedges and serve.

INGREDIENTS

1½ cups all-purpose flour, plus more as needed

¾ cup boiling water

7 tablespoons canola oil

1 tablespoon toasted sesame oil

1 teaspoon kosher salt

4 scallions, trimmed and sliced thin

YIELD: 4 TO 6 SERVINGS
ACTIVE TIME: 10 MINUTES
TOTAL TIME: 25 MINUTES

TEQUILA CHEESE DIP

INGREDIENTS

6 oz. Oaxaca cheese, cubed

½ plum tomato, diced

¼ white onion, diced

2 tablespoons diced green chile peppers

2 tablespoons sugar

¼ cup fresh lime juice

1 teaspoon chili powder

1 oz. tequila

Tortilla chips, for serving

DIRECTIONS

1   Preheat the oven to 350°F. Place the cheese, tomato, onion, and chiles in a small cast-iron skillet and stir to combine. Set the mixture aside.

2   Combine the sugar, lime juice, and chili powder in a small saucepan and cook over medium heat, stirring to dissolve the sugar, until the mixture is syrupy.

3   Drizzle the syrup over the cheese mixture, place the skillet in the oven, and bake until the cheese has melted and is golden brown on top, about 15 minutes.

4   Remove the pan from the oven, pour the tequila over the mixture, and use a long match or a wand lighter to ignite it. Bring the flaming skillet to the table and enjoy with tortilla chips once the flames have gone out.

YIELD: 4 SERVINGS
ACTIVE TIME: 30 MINUTES
TOTAL TIME: 2 HOURS

FALAFEL

INGREDIENTS

1 (14 oz.) can of chickpeas, drained and rinsed

½ red onion, chopped

1 cup fresh parsley, chopped

1 cup fresh cilantro, chopped

3 bunches of scallions, trimmed and chopped

1 jalapeño chile pepper, stem and seeds removed, chopped

3 garlic cloves

1 teaspoon cumin

1 teaspoon kosher salt, plus more to taste

½ teaspoon cardamom

¼ teaspoon black pepper

2 tablespoons chickpea flour

½ teaspoon baking soda

Canola oil, as needed

Hummus, for serving

DIRECTIONS

1   Line a baking sheet with parchment paper. Place all of the ingredients, except for the canola oil and hummus, in a food processor and blitz until pureed.

2   Scoop ¼-cup portions of the puree onto the baking sheet and chill the falafel in the refrigerator for 1 hour.

3   Add canola oil to a cast-iron Dutch oven until it is 2 inches deep and warm it to 325°F over medium heat.

4   Working in batches, add the falafel to the oil and fry them, turning as needed, until they are golden brown, about 6 minutes. Transfer the cooked falafel to a paper towel–lined plate to drain.

5   When all of the falafel have been cooked, serve with hummus.

FALAFEL, SEE PAGE 51

YIELD: 6 SERVINGS
ACTIVE TIME: 25 MINUTES
TOTAL TIME: 45 MINUTES

CRAB RANGOON

INGREDIENTS

1 lb. cream cheese, softened

6 oz. fresh crabmeat

2 tablespoons confectioners' sugar

¼ teaspoon kosher salt

40 wonton wrappers

Canola oil, as needed

DIRECTIONS

1 Place the cream cheese, crabmeat, sugar, and salt in a medium bowl and fold until the mixture is combined.

2 Place 1 tablespoon of the mixture in the middle of a wrapper. Rub the wrapper's edge with a wet finger, bring the corners together, pinch to seal tightly, and transfer to a parchment-lined baking sheet. Repeat with the remaining wrappers and filling.

3 Add canola oil to a cast-iron Dutch oven until it is 2 inches deep and warm it to 325°F over medium heat. Working in batches, gently slip the wontons into the hot oil and fry, while turning, until golden all over, about 3 minutes. Transfer the cooked dumplings to a paper towel–lined wire rack and let them cool briefly before enjoying.

YIELD: 4 SERVINGS

ACTIVE TIME: 5 MINUTES

TOTAL TIME: 25 MINUTES

BAKED CAMEMBERT

INGREDIENTS

1 wheel of Camembert cheese

1 cup granola

½ cup maple syrup

DIRECTIONS

1 Preheat the oven to 350°F. Place the Camembert in a small cast-iron skillet. Sprinkle the granola over the cheese and drizzle the maple syrup on top.

2 Place the pan in the oven and bake the cheese until it has softened and is warmed through, about 10 minutes. Remove from the oven and serve immediately.

YIELD: 4 SERVINGS
ACTIVE TIME: 20 MINUTES
TOTAL TIME: 50 MINUTES

FRIED SQUASH BLOSSOMS

INGREDIENTS

10 squash blossoms, stamens removed

1 bunch of fresh spearmint

2 cups shredded queso fresco

Zest and juice of 1 lemon

Salt, to taste

1 cup all-purpose flour

1 teaspoon baking powder

2 egg yolks

1 cup seltzer water

2 cups canola oil

DIRECTIONS

1 Place the squash blossoms on a paper towel–lined baking sheet.

2 Finely chop the spearmint and combine it with the queso fresco. Add the lemon zest and juice, season the mixture with the salt, and stir to combine.

3 Stuff the squash blossoms with the mixture, taking care not to tear the flowers.

4 In a small bowl, combine the flour, baking powder, egg yolks, and seltzer water and work the mixture with a whisk until it is a smooth batter. Let the batter rest for 20 minutes.

5 Place the canola oil in a large, deep cast-iron skillet and warm it to 350°F over medium heat.

6 Fold the tips of the squash blossoms closed and dip them into the batter. Gently slip them into the canola oil and fry until crispy and golden brown all over, about 2 minutes, making sure you only turn the squash blossoms once.

7 Drain the fried squash blossoms on the baking sheet. Season them lightly with salt and enjoy.

YIELD: 4 SERVINGS
ACTIVE TIME: 20 MINUTES
TOTAL TIME: 35 MINUTES

VEGETARIAN TAQUITOS

INGREDIENTS

2 poblano chile peppers

2 cups ricotta cheese

Salt, to taste

8 corn tortillas

¼ cup extra-virgin olive oil

DIRECTIONS

1   Roast the poblanos over an open flame, on the grill, or in the oven until they are charred all over. Place the poblanos in a bowl, cover the bowl with plastic wrap, and let the chiles steam for 10 minutes. When cool enough to handle, remove the skins, seeds, and stems from the poblanos and dice the remaining flesh.

2   Stir the poblanos into the ricotta, season the mixture with salt, and set the mixture aside.

3   Place the tortillas in a large, dry cast-iron skillet and warm them for 30 seconds on each side. Fill the tortillas with the cheese-and-poblano mixture and roll them up tight, tucking in the ends of the tortillas so that the taquitos do not come apart.

4   Place the olive oil in the skillet and warm it over medium heat. Place the tortillas in the pan, seam side down, and cook for 1 minute before turning them over. Cook the taquitos until browned all over, about 5 minutes.

5   Transfer the taquitos to a paper towel–lined plate and let them drain before enjoying.

YIELD: 4 SERVINGS
ACTIVE TIME: 25 MINUTES
TOTAL TIME: 30 MINUTES

SAUTÉED RED CABBAGE WITH APPLES, FENNEL & BALSAMIC

INGREDIENTS

½ head of red cabbage, core removed, sliced

3 tablespoons unsalted butter

1 apple, peel and core removed, diced

1 teaspoon fennel seeds

Salt and pepper, to taste

1 tablespoon balsamic vinegar

DIRECTIONS

1   Place the cabbage, 1 tablespoon of the butter, and ¼ cup of water in a large cast-iron skillet. Bring the water to a boil and cover the pan with a lid. Steam the cabbage until the thick ribs are tender, 5 to 8 minutes. Remove the lid and cook until the water has evaporated.

2   Add the remaining butter, apple, and fennel seeds, season the mixture with salt and pepper, and reduce the heat to medium-low. Cook, stirring occasionally, until the cabbage and apple have caramelized, about 10 minutes.

3   Stir in the balsamic vinegar, cook for another minute, and enjoy.

STIR-FRIED BOK CHOY

INGREDIENTS

1 tablespoon avocado oil

½ lb. bok choy, sliced

1 tablespoon mirin

1 teaspoon soy sauce

Salt, to taste

DIRECTIONS

1 Place the avocado oil in a large cast-iron skillet and warm it over medium-high heat. Add the bok choy and cook, stirring occasionally, until the greens have wilted, about 5 minutes.

2 Stir in the mirin and soy sauce and cook the bok choy for 1 more minute.

3 Season the bok choy with salt and enjoy.

YIELD: 4 SERVINGS
ACTIVE TIME: 10 MINUTES
TOTAL TIME: 20 MINUTES

LEMON CAULIFLOWER RICE

INGREDIENTS

1 head of cauliflower, chopped

2 tablespoons extra-virgin olive oil

Salt, to taste

3 tablespoons fresh lemon juice

2 teaspoons lemon zest

DIRECTIONS

1 Place the pieces of cauliflower in a food processor and blitz until they are granular.

2 Place the olive oil in a large cast-iron skillet and warm it over medium-high heat. Add the cauliflower and cook, stirring occasionally, until it starts to brown, about 8 minutes.

3 Season the cauliflower with salt, stir in the lemon juice and lemon zest, and cook, stirring occasionally, until the "rice" is fragrant and warmed through, about 4 minutes.

YIELD: 4 SERVINGS
ACTIVE TIME: 1 HOUR AND 30 MINUTES
TOTAL TIME: 3 HOURS

CHARRED SWEET POTATOES

INGREDIENTS

1½ lbs. small sweet potatoes, scrubbed

4 tablespoons unsalted butter

2 tablespoons honey

Salt, to taste

DIRECTIONS

1 Preheat the oven to 400°F and position a rack in the bottom third of the oven. Place the sweet potatoes in a large cast-iron skillet and poke them all over with a fork. Add just enough water to coat the bottom of the pan. Cover the pan tightly with aluminum foil, place it in the oven, and bake the sweet potatoes until fork-tender, 30 to 35 minutes.

2 Remove the sweet potatoes from the oven, place them on a cutting board, and let them cool.

3 Slice the sweet potatoes in half lengthwise.

4 Return the skillet to the oven and heat it for 20 minutes.

5 Remove the skillet from the oven, add 2 tablespoons of the butter, and swirl to coat the pan. Place the sweet potatoes in the pan, cut side down, place them in the oven, and roast until the edges are browned and crispy, 18 to 25 minutes.

6 While the sweet potatoes are in the oven, place the remaining butter and the honey in a small cast-iron skillet and warm the mixture over medium heat, stirring occasionally. Remove the pan from heat.

7 Remove the sweet potatoes from the oven and place them in a serving dish. Drizzle the honey butter over the sweet potatoes, season them with salt, and enjoy.

YIELD: 4 SERVINGS
ACTIVE TIME: 10 MINUTES
TOTAL TIME: 30 MINUTES

SEARED EGGPLANT

INGREDIENTS

1 cup wood chips

1 onion, quartered

2 teaspoons kosher salt

¼ cup avocado oil

1 small eggplant, trimmed and cubed

1 red bell pepper, stem and seeds removed, diced

¼ cup balsamic vinegar

DIRECTIONS

1   Place the wood chips in a small cast-iron skillet and light them on fire. Place the cast-iron pan into a roasting pan and place the onion beside the skillet. Cover the roasting pan with aluminum foil and smoke the onion for 20 minutes.

2   Transfer the onion to a food processor and puree until smooth. Add 1 teaspoon of the salt, stir to combine, and set the puree aside.

3   Place the avocado oil in a large cast-iron skillet and warm it over high heat. Add the eggplant, season it with the remaining salt, and sear it for 1 minute. Turn the eggplant over, add the bell pepper, and cook the mixture for another minute.

4   Add the balsamic vinegar and toss to coat.

5   To serve, spoon the onion puree onto the serving plates and top with the eggplant and pepper.

SEARED EGGPLANT, SEE PAGE 69

SPICY GREEN BEANS & SHIITAKES

INGREDIENTS

1 tablespoon avocado oil

½ lb. shiitake mushrooms

Salt, to taste

1 lb. green beans, cleaned and trimmed

1 tablespoon soy sauce

1 teaspoon sesame oil

½ teaspoon red pepper flakes

DIRECTIONS

1   Bring water to a boil in a medium saucepan and prepare an ice bath.

2   While the water is coming to a boil, place 1 tablespoon of the avocado oil in a large cast-iron skillet and warm it over medium heat. Add the mushrooms, season them with salt, and cook, stirring occasionally, until they start to brown, about 10 minutes. Remove the pan from heat.

3   Add salt and the green beans to the boiling water and parboil the green beans for 2 minutes. Drain the green beans and plunge them into the ice bath. Drain the green beans again and pat them dry.

4   Add the remaining avocado oil and the green beans to the skillet and cook, stirring occasionally, until the green beans start to brown and the mushrooms are well browned, about 5 minutes.

5   Remove the pan from heat and add the soy sauce, sesame oil, and red pepper flakes. Toss to combine and enjoy.

YIELD: 4 TO 6 SERVINGS

ACTIVE TIME: 5 MINUTES

TOTAL TIME: 1 HOUR

NEW POTATO CONFIT

INGREDIENTS

4 cups canola oil

5 lbs. new potatoes

Salt and pepper, to taste

DIRECTIONS

1 Place the canola oil in a cast-iron Dutch oven and warm it to 200°F over medium heat.

2 While the oil is warming, rinse and scrub the potatoes and then pat them dry. Carefully slip the potatoes into the warm oil and cook until fork-tender, about 1 hour.

3 Drain the potatoes, season generously with salt and pepper, and stir to ensure that the potatoes are evenly coated. Enjoy warm or at room temperature.

YIELD: 8 SERVINGS
ACTIVE TIME: 20 MINUTES
TOTAL TIME: 1 HOUR

BRAISED LEEKS

INGREDIENTS

½ cup extra-virgin olive oil

6 large leeks, trimmed, rinsed well, and halved lengthwise

Salt and pepper, to taste

2 tablespoons avocado oil

4 shallots, chopped

2 garlic cloves, minced

1 teaspoon dried thyme

1 teaspoon lemon zest

½ cup white wine

2 cups vegetable stock

DIRECTIONS

1 Preheat the oven to 400°F. Place the olive oil in a large cast-iron skillet and warm it over medium-high heat. Season the leeks with salt and pepper, place them in the pan, cut sides down, and sear until golden brown, about 5 minutes.

2 Season the leeks with salt and pepper, turn them over, and cook until browned on that side, about 2 minutes. Transfer the leeks to a bowl and set them aside.

3 Place the avocado oil in the skillet and warm it over medium-high heat. Add the shallots and cook, stirring frequently, until they start to brown, about 5 minutes.

4 Add the garlic, thyme, lemon zest, salt, and pepper to the pan and cook, stirring continually, for 1 minute.

5 Add the wine and cook until it has reduced by half, about 10 minutes.

6 Return the leeks to the skillet, add stock until they are almost, but not quite, submerged, and bring the mixture to a boil.

7 Place the skillet in the oven and braise the leeks until tender, about 30 minutes.

8 Remove the pan from the oven, transfer the leeks and braising liquid to a serving dish, and enjoy.

YIELD: 4 SERVINGS
ACTIVE TIME: 10 MINUTES
TOTAL TIME: 25 MINUTES

KALE WITH GARLIC, RAISINS & LEMON

INGREDIENTS

1 tablespoon extra-virgin olive oil

½ lb. kale, stems removed, chopped

2 garlic cloves, minced

¼ cup raisins

Salt and pepper, to taste

2 lemon wedges

DIRECTIONS

1 Place the olive oil in a large cast-iron skillet and warm it over medium-high heat. Add the kale and cook, stirring occasionally, for 5 minutes.

2 Add the garlic and cook, stirring continually, for 1 minute. Add the raisins and then deglaze the pan with ¼ cup water, scraping up any browned bits from the bottom of the pan. Cook until the water has evaporated and the kale is tender, about 5 minutes.

3 Season the dish with salt and pepper, squeeze the lemon wedges over it, and enjoy.

YIELD: 2 SERVINGS
ACTIVE TIME: 10 MINUTES
TOTAL TIME: 20 MINUTES

PEPPERY GLAZED ASPARAGUS

INGREDIENTS

Juice of 1 lemon

1 tablespoon sugar

1 tablespoon extra-virgin olive oil

1 teaspoon kosher salt

2 garlic cloves, minced

10 asparagus stalks, trimmed

1 teaspoon black pepper

Parmesan cheese, shaved, for garnish

DIRECTIONS

1   Preheat the broiler on the oven to high. Place the lemon juice, sugar, olive oil, salt, and garlic in a bowl, stir until well combined, and then add the asparagus. Toss until the asparagus is coated.

2   Place the asparagus in a large cast-iron skillet and sprinkle the pepper over it. Place the pan in the oven and broil until the asparagus is beautifully browned, about 10 minutes, turning it as necessary.

3   Remove the asparagus from the oven, garnish with the Parmesan, and enjoy.

PEPPERY GLAZED ASPARAGUS, SEE PAGE 79

TAHINI & YOGURT SAUCE

Place ¾ cup plain Greek yogurt, 1 minced garlic clove, 2 tablespoons tahini paste, the juice of 1 lemon, and ½ teaspoon cumin in a small bowl and whisk to combine. Season the sauce with salt and pepper, add 1 tablespoon sesame seeds and 1 tablespoon extra-virgin olive oil, and stir until incorporated. Use immediately or store in the refrigerator until needed.

YIELD: 4 SERVINGS
ACTIVE TIME: 20 MINUTES
TOTAL TIME: 1 HOUR

MUJADARA

INGREDIENTS

4 garlic cloves, minced

2 bay leaves

1 tablespoon cumin

Salt and pepper, to taste

1 cup basmati rice

1 cup brown or green lentils

⅓ cup extra-virgin olive oil

2 onions, halved and sliced thin

½ cup sliced scallions

½ cup chopped fresh cilantro

Tahini & Yogurt Sauce
(see sidebar), for serving

DIRECTIONS

1   Place the garlic, bay leaves, cumin, and a few generous pinches of salt in a cast-iron Dutch oven. Season with pepper, add 5 cups water, and bring to a boil over high heat.

2   Stir in the rice and reduce the heat to medium. Cover the pot and cook, stirring occasionally, for 10 minutes.

3   Add the lentils, return the mixture to a simmer, and cover the pot. Cook until the lentils are tender and the rice has absorbed all of the liquid, about 20 minutes.

4   Place the olive oil in a large cast-iron skillet and warm it over medium-high heat. Add the onions and cook, stirring frequently, until they are deeply caramelized, about 20 minutes. Remove the onions from the pan with a slotted spoon and transfer them to a paper towel–lined plate. Season with salt and pepper and set the onions aside.

5   Uncover the Dutch oven, remove the bay leaves, and discard them. Stir half of the scallions and the cilantro into the rice mixture. Season with salt and pepper, transfer to a serving dish, and top with the caramelized onions and the remaining scallions. Serve with the Tahini & Yogurt Sauce and enjoy.

YIELD: 6 SERVINGS

ACTIVE TIME: 30 MINUTES

TOTAL TIME: 24 HOURS

CHARRED ESCABECHE

INGREDIENTS

3½ tablespoons water

2½ tablespoons apple cider vinegar

¼ cup white vinegar

1 tablespoon sugar

1 tablespoon kosher salt

2 sprigs of fresh thyme

2 garlic cloves

2 bay leaves

5 oz. jalapeño chile peppers, halved

1½ lbs. carrots, peeled and sliced on a bias

DIRECTIONS

1 Place the water, vinegars, sugar, and salt in a saucepan and bring the mixture to a boil, stirring to dissolve the sugar and salt. Pour the brine into a large mason jar and add the thyme, garlic, and bay leaves.

2 Warm a large cast-iron skillet over high heat for 5 minutes.

3 Spray the skillet with nonstick cooking spray and add the jalapeños. Weigh them down with a smaller cast-iron skillet and cook until charred, about 5 minutes.

4 Place the jalapeños in the brine, add the carrots to the large skillet, and weigh them down with the smaller pan. Cook until charred, add them to the brine, and let the mixture cool to room temperature before covering and storing in the refrigerator. Chill for at least 1 day before serving.

YIELD: 4 SERVINGS
ACTIVE TIME: 15 MINUTES
TOTAL TIME: 15 MINUTES

FRIED BRUSSELS SPROUTS

INGREDIENTS

Canola oil, as needed

3 cups small Brussels sprouts, trimmed

2 tablespoons Tahini & Yogurt Sauce (see page 82)

½ cup crumbled feta cheese

Pinch of kosher salt

DIRECTIONS

1   Add canola oil to a cast-iron Dutch oven until it is about 2 inches deep and warm it to 350°F.

2   Gently slip the Brussels sprouts into the oil, working in batches to avoid crowding the pot. Fry the Brussels sprouts until golden brown, about 4 minutes, turning them as necessary. Remove one Brussels sprout to test that it is done—let it cool briefly and see if the inside is tender enough. Transfer the fried Brussels sprouts to a paper towel–lined plate.

3   Place the Brussels sprouts, tahini sauce, and feta in a mixing bowl and toss until combined. Sprinkle the salt over the dish and enjoy.

FRIED BRUSSELS SPROUTS, SEE PAGE 85

YIELD: 2 SERVINGS
ACTIVE TIME: 15 MINUTES
TOTAL TIME: 15 MINUTES

SPICY CARROTS

INGREDIENTS

2 large carrots, peeled

1 tablespoon avocado oil

1 tablespoon ras el hanout

2 teaspoons tahini paste

2 teaspoons honey

Sesame seeds, for garnish

DIRECTIONS

1 Cut the carrots into matchsticks that are approximately ½ inch wide and 3 inches long.

2 Place the avocado oil in a large cast-iron skillet and warm it over high heat. Add the carrots to the pan, making sure to leave as much space between them as possible.

3 Sprinkle the ras el hanout over the carrots and sear them until lightly charred all over, about 6 minutes, turning them as necessary.

4 Transfer the carrots to a paper towel–lined plate to drain.

5 Divide the carrots between the serving plates and drizzle the tahini and honey over each portion. Garnish with the sesame seeds and enjoy.

YIELD: 1½ CUPS

ACTIVE TIME: 20 MINUTES

TOTAL TIME: 30 MINUTES

SALSA VERDE

INGREDIENTS

1 lb. tomatillos, husks removed, rinsed

5 garlic cloves, unpeeled

1 small white onion, quartered

10 serrano chile peppers

2 bunches of fresh cilantro

Salt, to taste

DIRECTIONS

1 Warm a large cast-iron skillet over high heat. Place the tomatillos, garlic, onion, and chiles in the pan and cook until charred all over, turning them occasionally.

2 Remove the vegetables from the pan and let them cool slightly.

3 Peel the garlic cloves and remove the stems and seeds from the chiles. Place the charred vegetables in a blender, add the cilantro, and puree until smooth.

4 Season the salsa with salt and enjoy.

ENTREES

It's likely that whatever warm feelings you have for cast iron are tied to one of the preparations in this section, for the main course is where cast-iron cookware's versatility really shines. Worried that the thickness of a steak has kept the inside a little too rare for your liking? Simply slide the skillet into the oven. Has the weather turned and wiped out your plans to spend the afternoon grilling? Sear that beautiful piece of salmon and then stick it underneath the broiler to crisp up and lightly char the skin. Craving a comforting stew? Pile your ingredients in a Dutch oven and sit back with a glass of wine as your home fills with enticing aromas. Simply put, cast iron seems to supply an answer in every situation that can arise during the most critical time of the day—getting dinner on the table for yourself and your loved ones.

YIELD: 2 TO 4 SERVINGS
ACTIVE TIME: 30 MINUTES
TOTAL TIME: 2 HOURS

SKILLET SHISH KEBABS

INGREDIENTS

¾ cup extra-virgin olive oil

¼ cup fresh mint leaves

2 teaspoons chopped fresh rosemary

2 garlic cloves, smashed

1 teaspoon kosher salt, plus more to taste

Zest and juice of 1 lemon

¼ teaspoon black pepper, plus more to taste

2 lbs. boneless leg of lamb, trimmed and cut into 1-inch cubes

1 zucchini, cut into 1-inch cubes

1 summer squash, cut into 1-inch cubes

1 red bell pepper, stem and seeds removed, cut into 1-inch cubes

1 green bell pepper, stem and seeds removed, cut into 1-inch cubes

2 red onions, cut into 1-inch cubes

DIRECTIONS

1 Place ½ cup of the olive oil, the mint, rosemary, garlic, salt, lemon zest, lemon juice, and pepper in a blender and puree until smooth.

2 Place the lamb in a bowl, add half of the marinade, and toss to coat. Cover the bowl with plastic wrap, place the lamb in the refrigerator, and marinate for 1 hour, stirring every 15 minutes.

3 Place the vegetables in another bowl, add the remaining marinade, and toss to coat. Cover the bowl with plastic wrap and let the vegetables marinate at room temperature for 1 hour.

4 Preheat the oven to 350°F. Thread the lamb onto skewers, making sure to leave a bit of space between each piece. Thread the vegetable mixture onto skewers, making sure to alternate between the vegetables.

5 Place the skewers in a 13 x 9–inch baking dish and pour the marinade over them. Cover the dish and let the skewers marinate at room temperature for 30 minutes.

6 Remove the skewers from the marinade and pat them dry. Place 2 tablespoons of the olive oil in a large cast-iron skillet and warm it over medium-high heat. Add the vegetable skewers to the pan and cook until golden brown all over, about 5 minutes, turning them as necessary.

7 Transfer the skillet to the oven and roast the vegetables until they are tender, 8 to 10 minutes. Remove the pan from the oven and set the vegetable skewers aside.

8 Place the remaining olive oil in the skillet and warm it over medium-high heat. Add the lamb kebabs and cook until they are browned all over and medium-rare (internal temperature of 120°F), about 8 minutes, turning them as necessary. Let the cooked lamb rest for 5 minutes before serving.

YIELD: 2 SERVINGS
ACTIVE TIME: 15 MINUTES
TOTAL TIME: 30 MINUTES

THE ULTIMATE THANKSGIVING LEFTOVERS SANDWICH

INGREDIENTS

1 tablespoon mayonnaise

1 tablespoon leftover gravy

Salt and pepper, to taste

2 tablespoons unsalted butter, softened

4 slices of bread

¼ cup leftover stuffing

4 oz. leftover turkey, sliced

1 tablespoon cranberry sauce

DIRECTIONS

1 Place the mayonnaise and gravy in a mixing bowl, season the mixture with salt and pepper, and stir to combine. Set the mixture aside.

2 Warm a large cast-iron skillet over medium heat. Spread the butter on one side of each slice of bread. Place two slices of the bread, buttered sides down, in the skillet and top them with equal parts of the gravy mixture, stuffing, and turkey.

3 Spread the cranberry sauce on the unbuttered sides of the two remaining bread slices and set them on top of the turkey.

4 When the buttered sides of the bread are golden brown, flip the sandwich over. Cook until that side is also golden brown and enjoy.

YIELD: 4 SERVINGS
ACTIVE TIME: 20 MINUTES
TOTAL TIME: 1 HOUR AND 20 MINUTES

POMEGRANATE & HONEY-GLAZED CHICKEN

INGREDIENTS

¼ cup avocado oil

1 large onion, chopped

3 garlic cloves, minced

½ cup pomegranate molasses

½ cup sweetened pomegranate juice

½ cup honey

2 cups vegetable or chicken stock

1 teaspoon cumin

½ teaspoon ground ginger

⅛ teaspoon allspice

½ teaspoon turmeric

4 lbs. bone-in, skin-on chicken pieces

Salt and pepper, to taste

Fresh parsley, chopped, for garnish

Pomegranate seeds, for garnish

DIRECTIONS

1 Place 2 tablespoons of the avocado oil in a large cast-iron skillet and warm it over medium-high heat. Add the onion and cook, stirring occasionally, until it is soft and translucent, about 3 minutes.

2 Add the garlic and cook, stirring frequently, until fragrant, about 1 minute. Stir in the pomegranate molasses, pomegranate juice, honey, stock, and seasonings and bring the mixture to a boil. Lower the heat and simmer the sauce until it has reduced by half and thickened slightly, about 20 minutes.

3 Taste the sauce and adjust the seasoning as necessary. Transfer the sauce to a bowl and set it aside.

4 Rinse the chicken pieces, pat them dry, and season with salt and pepper.

5 Place the remaining avocado oil in the pan. Add the chicken pieces, skin side down, and cook until browned. Turn the chicken over, pour the sauce into the pan, reduce the heat, and cover the pan. Cook the chicken until it is cooked through and tender, 35 to 40 minutes.

6 Transfer the cooked chicken to a platter, garnish with parsley and pomegranate seeds, and enjoy.

EDAMAME SUCCOTASH

INGREDIENTS

4 slices of thick-cut bacon

2 tablespoons unsalted butter

1 red onion, minced

4 cups canned corn

1 red bell pepper, stem and seeds removed, diced

2 cups edamame

Salt and pepper, to taste

1 tablespoon chopped fresh marjoram

¼ cup chopped fresh basil

DIRECTIONS

1   Place a large cast-iron skillet over medium heat, add the bacon, and cook until crispy, about 8 minutes, turning it as necessary. Remove the bacon from the pan and place it on a paper towel–lined plate to drain. When it is cool enough to handle, crumble the bacon into bite-size pieces.

2   Place the butter in the skillet and melt it over medium-high heat. Add the onion and cook, stirring occasionally, until it is translucent, about 3 minutes.

3   Add the corn, bell pepper, and edamame and cook, stirring frequently, until the corn is tender, about 3 minutes.

4   Season the mixture with salt and pepper, stir in the marjoram, basil, and crumbled bacon, and enjoy.

YIELD: 2 SERVINGS
ACTIVE TIME: 20 MINUTES
TOTAL TIME: 40 MINUTES

WHOLE BRANZINO

INGREDIENTS

1 to 2 lb. whole branzino

2 fresh basil leaves

1 tablespoon kosher salt

1 tablespoon black pepper

2 tablespoons extra-virgin olive oil

½ lemon

DIRECTIONS

1   Preheat the oven to 425°F. Clean the fish, remove the bones, and descale it. Pat the fish dry with paper towels and rub the inside with the basil leaves. Season it with the salt and pepper and close the fish back up.

2   Place the olive oil in a large cast-iron skillet and warm it over high heat. Place the fish in the pan and cook until it is browned on both sides, 8 to 10 minutes.

3   Place the pan in the oven and roast the fish until the internal temperature is 145°F, about 10 minutes.

4   Remove the pan from the oven and transfer the branzino to a large platter. Squeeze the lemon over the top and enjoy.

WHOLE BRANZINO, SEE PAGE 101

YIELD: 4 SERVINGS

ACTIVE TIME: 30 MINUTES

TOTAL TIME: 1 HOUR

PORK & APPLE CASSEROLE

INGREDIENTS

8 apples, cored and sliced

2 teaspoons cinnamon

1 teaspoon freshly
grated nutmeg

¼ cup sugar

¼ cup all-purpose flour

Salt and pepper, to taste

¼ cup apple cider

1½ lb. pork tenderloin

2 tablespoons freshly
ground rosemary

2 tablespoons freshly
ground thyme

DIRECTIONS

1   Preheat the oven to 325°F. Place the apples, cinnamon, nutmeg, sugar, flour, and a pinch of salt in a mixing bowl and stir to combine. Transfer the mixture to a cast-iron Dutch oven and then add the apple cider.

2   Rub the pork tenderloin with the ground herbs, pepper, and a pinch of salt. Place the pork on top of the apple mixture, cover the Dutch oven, and place it in the oven. Braise the tenderloin until a meat thermometer inserted into its center registers 145°F, about 40 minutes.

3   Remove the pork tenderloin from the oven and let it rest for 10 minutes. Slice it thin and serve the slices on beds of the apple mixture.

YIELD: 4 SERVINGS

ACTIVE TIME: 15 MINUTES

TOTAL TIME: 15 MINUTES

FUL MEDAMES

INGREDIENTS

1 tablespoon avocado oil

1 onion, chopped

3 garlic cloves, minced

2 tomatoes, chopped

2 (14 oz.) cans of fava beans, drained and rinsed

1 teaspoon cumin

1 tablespoon ras el hanout

¼ teaspoon cayenne pepper

3 tablespoons fresh lemon juice

¼ cup fresh parsley, chopped

Salt, to taste

DIRECTIONS

1   Place the avocado oil in a large cast-iron skillet and warm it over medium heat. Add the onion and garlic and cook, stirring frequently, until the onion is translucent, about 3 minutes.

2   Add the tomatoes and cook for 2 minutes, stirring occasionally. Stir in the fava beans, cumin, ras el hanout, and cayenne pepper and cook until the flavor has developed, 6 to 8 minutes.

3   Remove the pan from the heat and mash the fava beans lightly, right in the skillet, until most of the beans are mashed. Scoop the ful medames into a serving bowl, stir in the lemon juice and parsley, season the dish with salt, and enjoy.

FUL MEDAMES, SEE PAGE 105

YIELD: 4 SERVINGS
ACTIVE TIME: 20 MINUTES
TOTAL TIME: 20 MINUTES

LAMB, SZECHUAN STYLE

INGREDIENTS

3 tablespoons cumin seeds

2 teaspoons Szechuan peppercorns

1 teaspoon kosher salt

3 tablespoons canola oil

4 dried red chile peppers, stems and seeds removed, torn

2 teaspoons red pepper flakes

1½ lbs. boneless leg of lamb, cubed

1 yellow onion, sliced

2 scallions, trimmed and sliced thin, for garnish

Fresh cilantro, chopped, for garnish

White rice, cooked, for serving

DIRECTIONS

1   Place the cumin seeds and Szechuan peppercorns in a large, dry cast-iron skillet and toast them over medium heat for 1 minute. Remove the mixture from the pan and grind to a fine powder with a mortar and pestle.

2   Place the salt, 2 tablespoons of the canola oil, the dried chilies, red pepper flakes, and toasted spice mixture in a large bowl and stir to combine. Add the lamb pieces and toss until they are coated.

3   Add the remaining canola oil to the large cast-iron skillet and warm it over high heat. Add the lamb and onion and cook, stirring occasionally, until the lamb is browned all over and medium-rare, 6 to 8 minutes.

4   Garnish the dish with scallions and cilantro and serve it with white rice.

YIELD: 4 SERVINGS

ACTIVE TIME: 15 MINUTES

TOTAL TIME: 15 MINUTES

SHRIMP CURRY

INGREDIENTS

16 large shrimp, shells removed, deveined

1 cup unsweetened shredded coconut

1 teaspoon cumin seeds

3 chiles de arbol, stems removed

2 large tomatoes, chopped

¼ cup canola oil

5 whole cloves

4 green cardamom pods

2 bay leaves

1 cinnamon stick

1 yellow onion, chopped

1 tablespoon coriander

1 teaspoon turmeric

1 teaspoon black pepper

2 garlic cloves, mashed

1 teaspoon grated fresh ginger

1 (14 oz.) can of coconut milk

½ cup water

2 tablespoons brown sugar

2 serrano chile peppers, stems and seeds removed, sliced thin

1 cup chopped fresh cilantro

Salt, to taste

DIRECTIONS

1   Place 4 of the shrimp, the coconut, cumin seeds, chiles de arbol, tomatoes, and canola oil in a food processor and blitz until the mixture is a paste.

2   Place the cloves, cardamom pods, bay leaves, and cinnamon stick in a large, dry cast-iron skillet and toast the mixture over medium heat for 1 minute, shaking the pan frequently. Stir in the onion, coriander, turmeric, black pepper, garlic, and ginger. Cook for 1 minute, add the shrimp paste, and stir to combine. Cook, stirring frequently, for 3 minutes.

3   Add the coconut milk and water and bring to a boil. Add the brown sugar and serrano peppers, stir to incorporate, and cook for another minute.

4   Reduce the heat, add the remaining shrimp and the cilantro, and simmer until the shrimp are pink and the sauce has thickened slightly, 2 to 4 minutes.

5   Season with salt and ladle the curry into warmed bowls.

YIELD: 4 SERVINGS

ACTIVE TIME: 30 MINUTES

TOTAL TIME: 2 HOURS AND 30 MINUTES

STEAK WITH PEPPERS & ONIONS

INGREDIENTS

½ cup extra-virgin olive oil

2 garlic cloves, minced

2 teaspoons Worcestershire sauce

2 teaspoons red wine vinegar

1 tablespoon Colman's mustard powder

2 lbs. sirloin tips, chopped

2 yellow onions, chopped

2 red bell peppers, stems and seeds removed, chopped

Salt and pepper, to taste

DIRECTIONS

1   Place 7 tablespoons of the olive oil in a large bowl. Add the garlic, Worcestershire sauce, red wine vinegar, and mustard powder and stir to combine. Add the sirloin tips and stir until they are coated. Cover and refrigerate for 2 hours, while stirring once or twice. If time allows, let the sirloin tips marinate overnight.

2   Place a large cast-iron skillet over medium-high heat and coat the bottom with the remaining olive oil. Add the sirloin tips and cook until they are browned all over, about 8 minutes, turning them as necessary. Remove the sirloin tips from the pan and set them aside.

3   Reduce the heat to medium, add the onions and bell peppers, and cook, without stirring, until they are browned, about 5 minutes. Return the sirloin tips to the pan and cook for another 2 minutes, until they are warmed through. Season with salt and pepper and serve immediately.

YIELD: 6 SERVINGS
ACTIVE TIME: 25 MINUTES
TOTAL TIME: 1 HOUR AND 15 MINUTES

JAMBALAYA

INGREDIENTS

½ lb. andouille sausage, sliced

½ lb. small shrimp, shells removed, deveined

¼ cup extra-virgin olive oil

4 boneless, skinless chicken thighs, chopped

2 yellow onions, chopped

1 large green bell pepper, stem and seeds removed, chopped

2 celery stalks, chopped

3 garlic cloves, minced

3 plum tomatoes, chopped

2 bay leaves

2 tablespoons paprika

2 tablespoons dried thyme

1 tablespoon garlic powder

1 tablespoon onion powder

1 teaspoon cayenne pepper

Salt and pepper, to taste

1½ cups long-grain white rice

2 tablespoons Worcestershire sauce

Hot sauce, to taste

3 cups chicken stock

Scallions, trimmed and chopped, for garnish

DIRECTIONS

1   Place the sausage in a cast-iron Dutch oven and cook it over medium-high heat until browned all over, about 8 minutes, turning it as necessary. Remove the sausage from the pot and set it aside.

2   Add the shrimp and cook them for 1 minute on each side. Remove the shrimp and set them aside.

3   Add the olive oil, chicken, onions, bell pepper, and celery to the Dutch oven. Cook until the vegetables start to caramelize and the chicken is browned and cooked through, 6 to 8 minutes. Add the garlic and cook until fragrant, about 2 minutes.

4   Add the tomatoes, the bay leaves, and all of the seasonings. Simmer for 30 minutes, stirring occasionally.

5   Stir in the rice, Worcestershire sauce, hot sauce, and stock. Return the sausage to the pot, reduce the heat to medium-low, cover the Dutch oven, and cook the jambalaya for 25 minutes.

6   Return the shrimp to the pot, cover it, and remove it from heat. Let it sit for 5 minutes, then ladle the jambalaya into bowls and garnish with the scallions.

YIELD: 4 SERVINGS
ACTIVE TIME: 30 MINUTES
TOTAL TIME: 24 HOURS

CHAMIN

DIRECTIONS

1 Preheat the oven to 250°F. Place the olive oil in a cast-iron Dutch oven and warm it over medium heat. Add the onion, garlic, parsnip, carrots, cumin, turmeric, and ginger and cook, stirring continually, for 2 minutes.

2 Add the brisket and lamb and cook, stirring occasionally, until both are browned all over, about 8 minutes.

3 Add the stock and bring the stew to a simmer. Stir in the chickpeas, potato, zucchini, tomatoes, lentils, bay leaf, and cilantro. Cover the pot, place it in the oven, and cook until the meat is tender, about 1 hour.

4 Remove the stew from the oven and skim the fat from the top. Season the stew with salt and pepper and ladle it into warmed bowls. Garnish with the chiles and serve with lemon wedges and rice.

INGREDIENTS

1½ tablespoons extra-virgin olive oil

1 small onion, chopped

5 garlic cloves, minced

¾ cup chopped parsnip

2 carrots, peeled and sliced

1 teaspoon cumin

¼ teaspoon turmeric

1½-inch piece of fresh ginger, peeled and minced

½ lb. beef brisket, trimmed and chopped

4 oz. lamb shoulder, trimmed and chopped

4 cups beef or chicken stock

½ cup chickpeas, soaked overnight and drained

1 small potato, peeled and chopped

1 small zucchini, sliced

½ lb. tomatoes, chopped

2 tablespoons brown lentils

1 bay leaf

½ bunch of fresh cilantro, chopped

Salt and pepper, to taste

Fresh chile peppers, stems and seeds removed, chopped, for garnish

Lemon wedges, for serving

Long-grain rice, cooked, for serving

YIELD: 6 SERVINGS
ACTIVE TIME: 25 MINUTES
TOTAL TIME: 40 MINUTES

ROMESCO DE PEIX

INGREDIENTS

½ cup slivered almonds

½ teaspoon saffron

½ cup extra-virgin olive oil

1 large yellow onion, chopped

2 large red bell peppers, stems and seeds removed, chopped

2½ teaspoons sweet paprika

1 tablespoon smoked paprika

1 bay leaf

2 tablespoons tomato paste

½ cup sherry

2 cups fish stock

1 (28 oz.) can of chopped tomatoes, with their liquid

Salt and pepper, to taste

1½ lbs. monkfish fillets, chopped into large pieces

1 lb. mussels, rinsed well and debearded

Fresh cilantro, finely chopped, for garnish

DIRECTIONS

1 Place the almonds in a large, dry cast-iron skillet and toast them over medium heat until they are just browned, shaking the pan occasionally. Transfer them to a food processor and pulse until they are finely ground.

2 Place the saffron and ¼ cup boiling water in a bowl and let the mixture steep.

3 Place the olive oil in a cast-iron Dutch oven and warm it over medium heat. Add the onion and bell peppers and cook, stirring occasionally, until the peppers are tender, about 15 minutes.

4 Add the sweet paprika, smoked paprika, bay leaf, and tomato paste and cook, stirring continually, for 1 minute. Add the sherry and bring the mixture to a boil. Boil for 5 minutes and then stir in the stock, tomatoes, saffron, and the soaking liquid. Stir to combine, season with salt and pepper, and reduce the heat so that the soup simmers.

5 Add the ground almonds and cook until the mixture thickens slightly, about 8 minutes. Add the fish and mussels, stir gently to incorporate, and simmer until the fish is cooked through and a majority of the mussels have opened, about 5 minutes. Discard any mussels that do not open.

6 Ladle the soup into warmed bowls, garnish each portion with cilantro, and enjoy.

YIELD: 4 SERVINGS

ACTIVE TIME: 15 MINUTES

TOTAL TIME: 30 MINUTES

FISH & CHIPS

INGREDIENTS

1 cup all-purpose flour

1 teaspoon baking powder

2 egg yolks

1 cup seltzer water

Canola oil, as needed

5 potatoes, sliced into long, thin strips

2 tablespoons chopped fresh rosemary

Salt, to taste

1½ lbs. pollock fillets

Lemon wedges, for serving

DIRECTIONS

1 In a small bowl, combine the flour, baking powder, egg yolks, and seltzer water and work the mixture with a whisk until it is a smooth batter. Let the batter rest for 20 minutes.

2 Add canola oil to a cast-iron Dutch oven until it is 2 inches deep and warm it to 350°F over medium-high heat. Place the sliced potatoes in the oil and fry until golden brown. Remove the fried potatoes with a slotted spoon and transfer to a paper towel–lined plate to drain.

3 Warm the oil back to 350°F. While the oil is warming, place the fried potatoes in a bowl, add the rosemary, season with salt, and toss to coat.

4 Dredge the pollock in the batter until it is coated all over.

5 Place the battered pollock in the oil and fry it is until golden brown and cooked through, about 5 minutes.

6 Serve the fried pollock with the fried potatoes and lemon wedges.

YIELD: 4 TO 6 SERVINGS

ACTIVE TIME: 30 MINUTES

TOTAL TIME: 4 HOURS

BRAISED LAMB WITH MINTY PEAS

INGREDIENTS

2 tablespoons extra-virgin olive oil

5 lb. bone-in lamb shoulder

Salt, to taste

1 small onion, diced

2 carrots, peeled and diced

3 bay leaves

2 tablespoons black peppercorns

2 cups water

2 sprigs of fresh rosemary

3 sprigs of fresh mint

3 cups peas

DIRECTIONS

1   Preheat the oven to 300°F. Place the olive oil in a cast-iron Dutch oven and warm it over medium-high heat. Season all sides of the lamb shoulder generously with salt. Place the lamb in the pot and cook until it is browned on all sides, about 8 minutes, turning it as necessary.

2   Place the onion, carrots, bay leaves, peppercorns, water, and rosemary in the Dutch oven. Cover the pot, place it in the oven, and braise the lamb until it is fork-tender, about 3½ hours.

3   When the lamb shoulder is close to being ready, place the sprigs of mint and peas in a saucepan and cover with water. Cook over medium heat until the peas are tender, approximately 4 minutes for fresh peas and 7 minutes if using frozen. Drain, discard the mint, and set the peas aside.

4   Remove the lamb shoulder from the oven and let it rest for 10 minutes before slicing and serving alongside the peas.

YIELD: 6 SERVINGS

ACTIVE TIME: 45 MINUTES

TOTAL TIME: 2 HOURS

BOLOGNESE WITH PENNE

INGREDIENTS

2 tablespoons extra-virgin olive oil

½ lb. bacon, chopped

1½ lbs. ground beef

Salt and pepper, to taste

1 onion, chopped

1 carrot, peeled and minced

3 celery stalks, chopped

2 garlic cloves, minced

1 tablespoon fresh thyme

2 cups sherry

8 cups crushed tomatoes

1 cup heavy cream

2 tablespoons finely chopped fresh sage

1 lb. penne

4 tablespoons unsalted butter

1 cup freshly grated Parmesan cheese, plus more for garnish

Fresh basil, for garnish

Red pepper flakes, for garnish (optional)

DIRECTIONS

1   Place the olive oil and bacon in a cast-iron Dutch oven and cook the bacon over medium heat until it is crispy, about 6 minutes. Add the beef, season with salt and pepper, and cook, breaking the beef up with a wooden spoon as it browns, until it is cooked through, about 8 minutes.

2   Remove the bacon and the beef from the pot and set them aside.

3   Add the onion, carrot, celery, and garlic to the Dutch oven, season the mixture with salt, and cook, stirring frequently, until the carrot is tender, about 8 minutes. Return the bacon and beef to the pan, add the thyme and sherry, and cook until the sherry has nearly evaporated.

4   Add the crushed tomatoes and 1 cup water, reduce the heat to low, and cook the sauce for approximately 45 minutes, stirring often, until it has thickened to the desired consistency.

5   Stir the cream and sage into the sauce and gently simmer for another 15 minutes.

6   Bring water to a boil in a large saucepan. Add salt and the penne and cook until it is just shy of al dente, about 6 minutes. Reserve 1 cup of the pasta water, drain the penne, and then return it to the pan. Add the butter, sauce, and reserved pasta water and stir to combine. Add the Parmesan and stir until it has melted.

7   Garnish the dish with additional Parmesan, basil, and red pepper flakes, if desired.

YIELD: 4 TO 6 SERVINGS
ACTIVE TIME: 20 MINUTES
TOTAL TIME: 40 MINUTES

LINGUINE WITH CLAM SAUCE

INGREDIENTS

Salt, to taste

1 lb. linguine

½ cup extra-virgin olive oil

3 garlic cloves, sliced thin

32 littleneck clams, scrubbed and rinsed well

1 cup white wine

1 cup clam juice

1 cup chopped parsley

¼ cup freshly grated Parmesan cheese

Salt and pepper, to taste

DIRECTIONS

1   Bring 4 quarts of water to a boil in a cast-iron Dutch oven. Add salt and the linguine and cook until the pasta is just short of al dente, about 6 minutes. Reserve ½ cup of the pasta water, drain the linguine, and set it aside.

2   Place the Dutch oven over medium heat. Add half of the olive oil and the garlic and cook, stirring continually, until the garlic starts to brown, about 2 minutes. Add the clams and wine, cover the pot, and cook until the majority of the clams have opened, 5 to 7 minutes. Use a slotted spoon to transfer the clams to a colander. Discard any clams that do not open.

3   Add the clam juice, parsley, and reserved pasta water to the Dutch oven. Cook, stirring occasionally, until the sauce starts to thicken, about 10 minutes. Remove all the clams from their shells and mince one-quarter of them.

4   Return the linguine to the pot. Add the Parmesan, season with salt and pepper, and stir until the cheese begins to melt.

5   Fold in the clams, drizzle the remaining olive oil over the dish, and enjoy.

YIELD: 6 SERVINGS

ACTIVE TIME: 30 MINUTES

TOTAL TIME: 45 MINUTES

SKILLET LASAGNA

INGREDIENTS

2 tablespoons extra-virgin olive oil

1 onion, sliced thin

4 garlic cloves, sliced thin

2 zucchini, chopped

1 cup chopped eggplant

2 cups baby spinach

1 (28 oz.) can of whole peeled San Marzano tomatoes, with their liquid, crushed by hand

Salt and pepper, to taste

8 sheets of no-cook lasagna

1 cup ricotta cheese

½ cup freshly grated Parmesan cheese, plus more for garnish

½ lb. fresh mozzarella cheese, sliced thin

Fresh basil, finely chopped, for garnish

DIRECTIONS

1   Place the olive oil in a large cast-iron skillet and warm it over medium-low heat. Add the onion and cook, stirring occasionally, until it has softened, about 5 minutes.

2   Add the garlic and cook, stirring continually, for 1 minute. Raise the heat to medium, add the zucchini and eggplant, and cook, stirring occasionally, until the zucchini has softened and the eggplant has collapsed, about 10 minutes.

3   Add the spinach and cook, stirring continually, until it has wilted, about 2 minutes. Transfer the vegetable mixture to a bowl.

4   Cover the bottom of the skillet with a thin layer of the tomatoes and season it with salt and pepper. Top with 4 sheets of lasagna, breaking off the edges as necessary to fit the pan. Spread half of the vegetable mixture over the lasagna and dot the mixture with dollops of ricotta. Top with one-third of the remaining tomatoes, season them with salt and pepper, and spread the remaining vegetable mixture over the top. Dot the vegetables with dollops of the remaining ricotta. Top with the remaining sheets of lasagna, spread the remaining tomatoes over the top, and then layer the Parmesan and mozzarella over the tomatoes.

5   Season with salt and pepper, cover the skillet, and cook over medium-low heat until the pasta is soft and the cheese has completely melted, 5 to 10 minutes.

6   Uncover the skillet, raise the heat to medium-high, and cook until the sauce has thickened, about 5 minutes. Remove the pan from heat and let the lasagna cool slightly, 5 to 10 minutes, before cutting. Sprinkle basil and more Parmesan over the lasagna and serve.

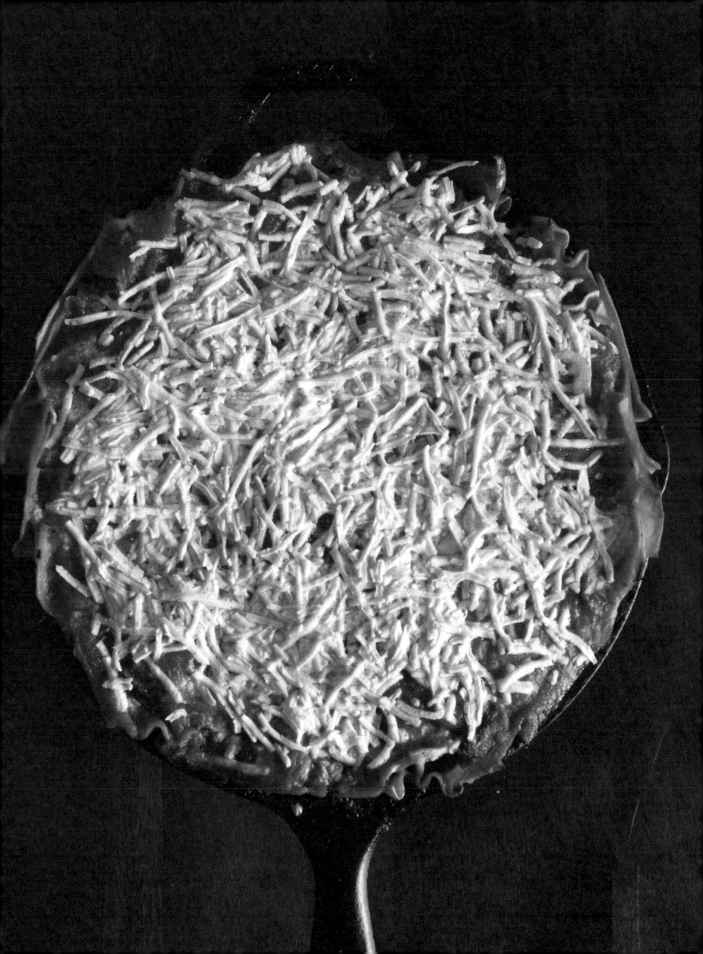

YIELD: 4 SERVINGS

ACTIVE TIME: 30 MINUTES

TOTAL TIME: 24 HOURS

ROASTED CHICKEN

INGREDIENTS

5 lb. whole chicken

Salt and pepper, to taste

2 tablespoons extra-virgin olive oil

1 tablespoon fresh thyme

1 tablespoon chopped fresh rosemary

DIRECTIONS

1 Place a wire rack in a rimmed baking sheet. Season the chicken generously inside and out with salt, place it on the wire rack, and chill it in the refrigerator overnight.

2 Remove the chicken from the refrigerator and pat it dry. Let the chicken sit at room temperature for 1 hour.

3 Preheat the oven to 500°F and place a large cast-iron skillet in the oven as it warms. Rub the olive oil over the chicken, season it with pepper, and sprinkle the thyme and rosemary over the top.

4 Carefully remove the skillet from the oven and place the chicken in the pan, breast side down. Place the chicken in the oven and roast for 15 minutes.

5 Turn the chicken over so that it is breast side up, lower the oven's temperature to 350°F, and roast the chicken until the juices run clear and the internal temperature in the thick part of a thigh is 160°F, about 35 minutes.

6 Remove the chicken from the oven, transfer it to a wire rack, and let it rest for 15 to 20 minutes before carving.

YIELD: 6 SERVINGS

ACTIVE TIME: 25 MINUTES

TOTAL TIME: 1 HOUR AND 15 MINUTES

SEARED SCALLOPS & SWEET CORN CHOWDER

INGREDIENTS

6 tablespoons unsalted butter

1 large onion, diced

6 slices of bacon, cooked and diced

2 celery stalks, chopped

2 garlic cloves, minced

¼ cup all-purpose flour

3 cups fresh corn kernels (from about 7 ears of corn)

3 sprigs of fresh thyme

2 large potatoes, peeled and diced

½ cup heavy cream

½ cup milk

Salt and pepper, to taste

1 tablespoon extra-virgin olive oil

6 fresh scallops

DIRECTIONS

1   Place the butter in a large cast-iron skillet and melt it over medium heat. Add the onion and cook, stirring occasionally, until it starts to brown, about 8 minutes.

2   Add the bacon, celery, and garlic and cook, stirring frequently, for 5 minutes.

3   Stir in the flour and then add the corn, thyme, potatoes, cream, and milk. Bring the chowder to a simmer, season it with salt and pepper, and cook until the potatoes are fork-tender, about 15 minutes.

4   Place the olive oil in a medium cast-iron skillet and warm it over medium-high heat.

5   Pat the scallops dry and season them with salt. Place the scallops in the pan and cook until golden brown on both sides, about 2 minutes per side.

6   Remove the sprigs of thyme from the chowder and discard them. Ladle the soup into warmed bowls and top each portion with a scallop.

YIELD: 6 SERVINGS

ACTIVE TIME: 30 MINUTES

TOTAL TIME: 1 HOUR AND 45 MINUTES

COTTAGE PIE

INGREDIENTS

6 russet potatoes, peeled and chopped

Salt and pepper, to taste

½ cup unsalted butter, divided into tablespoons

½ cup whole milk

¼ cup plain yogurt

1 tablespoon extra-virgin olive oil

½ yellow onion, minced

1 lb. ground beef

2 cups frozen peas

1 cup corn kernels

DIRECTIONS

1 Preheat the oven to 350°F. Place the potatoes in a large saucepan or pot and cover with cold water. Add salt and bring the water to a boil. Reduce the heat so that the water simmers and cook the potatoes until they are fork-tender, about 20 minutes.

2 Drain the potatoes and place them in a large bowl. Add 6 tablespoons of the butter, the milk, and yogurt and mash the potatoes until smooth. Season with salt and pepper and set aside.

3 Place the olive oil in a large cast-iron skillet and warm it over medium heat. Add the onion and cook, stirring occasionally, until it is translucent, about 3 minutes. Add the ground beef, season it with salt and pepper, and cook, while breaking it up with a wooden spoon, until browned, about 8 minutes. Drain some of the fat from the skillet and stir in the peas and corn.

4 Spread the mashed potatoes over the meat and vegetables and use a rubber spatula to smooth the top. Cut the remaining butter into slivers and dot the potatoes with them.

5 Cover the skillet with aluminum foil, place the pan in the oven, and bake the cottage pie for 30 minutes.

6 Remove the foil and bake the pie for another 10 minutes, until the potatoes start to turn golden brown. Remove the pie from the oven and let it cool for 5 minutes before serving.

YIELD: 4 SERVINGS

ACTIVE TIME: 35 MINUTES

TOTAL TIME: 1 HOUR

VEGETARIAN FRIED RICE

INGREDIENTS

2 tablespoons avocado oil, plus more as needed

½ lb. extra-firm tofu, drained and diced

3 tablespoons soy sauce

2 tablespoons rice vinegar

1 tablespoon sugar

1 shallot, diced

1 kohlrabi, peeled and diced

1-inch piece of fresh ginger, peeled and grated

2 cups leftover white rice

½ cup diced pineapple

¼ cup cashews

½ cup frozen peas

¼ cup chopped fresh cilantro, for garnish

Lime wedges, for serving

DIRECTIONS

1   Place 1 tablespoon of the avocado oil in a large cast-iron skillet and warm it over high heat. Add the tofu and cook, stirring frequently, until the tofu starts to brown, about 3 minutes.

2   Place 2 tablespoons of the soy sauce, 1 tablespoon of the vinegar, and the sugar in a small bowl and stir to combine. Pour this mixture over the tofu and cook until the liquid has reduced to a glaze. Transfer the tofu to a bowl and set it aside.

3   Add the shallot, kohlrabi, ginger, and remaining oil to the pan. Cook, stirring occasionally, for 2 minutes and then add the rice. It is very likely that the rice will stick to the bottom of the pan. Do your best to scrape it off with a spatula or wooden spoon. Cook the rice until it starts to brown, about 5 to 10 minutes, taking care not to let it become too mushy.

4   Stir in the remaining soy sauce and rice vinegar. Add the pineapple, cashews, frozen peas, and tofu to the pan. Gently fold to incorporate and cook until everything is warmed through, 2 to 3 minutes.

5   Taste, adjust the seasoning as necessary, and garnish the dish with the cilantro. Serve with lime wedges and enjoy.

YIELD: 4 SERVINGS

ACTIVE TIME: 15 MINUTES

TOTAL TIME: 50 MINUTES

STUFFED PEPPERS

INGREDIENTS

1½ cups chicken stock

¾ cup rice, rinsed and drained

½ lb. ground Italian sausage

2 onions, diced

6 garlic cloves, minced

½ teaspoon dried oregano

Salt and pepper, to taste

⅛ teaspoon red pepper flakes

1 (28 oz.) can of crushed tomatoes, drained

1¼ cups freshly grated Parmesan cheese

4 bell peppers, halved, seeds removed

Fresh herbs, chopped, for garnish

DIRECTIONS

1   Preheat the oven to 350°F. Place the stock and rice in a medium saucepan and bring it to a simmer over medium heat. Reduce the heat to low, cover the pan, and cook until the rice is almost tender and has absorbed all of the liquid, about 15 minutes.

2   Place the sausage in a large cast-iron skillet and cook it over medium-high heat until browned all over, about 8 minutes, breaking it up with a wooden spoon as it cooks. Using a slotted spoon, transfer the sausage to a large bowl.

3   Place the onions in the skillet and cook, stirring occasionally, until they are browned, 8 to 10 minutes. Stir in the garlic, oregano, salt, pepper, and red pepper flakes and cook, stirring continually, for 1 minute. Add the tomatoes, bring the mixture to a boil, and remove the pan from heat. Taste the sauce and adjust the seasoning as necessary.

4   Place 1 cup of the sauce and 1 cup of the Parmesan in the bowl with the sausage and stir until thoroughly combined. Fill the peppers with the mixture and sprinkle the remaining Parmesan over each one.

5   Place the stuffed peppers in the skillet, place the pan in the oven, and bake the peppers until they are tender, about 25 minutes. Warm the remaining sauce while the peppers are in the oven.

6   Remove the peppers from the oven, spoon some of the remaining sauce over each one, garnish with the fresh herbs, and enjoy.

YIELD: 2 SERVINGS

ACTIVE TIME: 15 MINUTES

TOTAL TIME: 15 MINUTES

CRISPY SALMON RICE

INGREDIENTS

2 tablespoons avocado oil

½ white onion, minced

¼ cup sliced scallions

¼ cup chopped fresh parsley

2 teaspoons kosher salt

2 cups leftover white rice

6 oz. salmon belly, chopped

1 tablespoon pomegranate molasses

1 tablespoon apple cider vinegar

DIRECTIONS

1   Place the avocado oil in a large cast-iron skillet and warm it over high heat. Add the onion, scallions, parsley, and salt and cook, stirring frequently, until the onion is translucent, about 2 minutes.

2   Add the rice and cook, stirring frequently, until the rice is crispy, about 3 minutes. Add the salmon, reduce the heat to medium-high, and cook until the salmon is cooked through, about 4 minutes.

3   Place the pomegranate molasses and vinegar in a small bowl and whisk to combine. Stir this mixture into the crispy rice, remove the pan from heat, and enjoy immediately.

YIELD: 4 SERVINGS

ACTIVE TIME: 15 MINUTES

TOTAL TIME: 15 MINUTES

BEEF & BROCCOLI STIR-FRY

INGREDIENTS

1 tablespoon avocado oil

2 garlic cloves, minced

1 lb. broccoli, cut into florets

¼ cup thinly sliced eggplant

1 lb. rib eye, sliced thin against the grain

Salt, to taste

¼ cup oyster sauce

2 tablespoons soy sauce

Chile peppers, sliced thin, for garnish

DIRECTIONS

1   Coat a large cast-iron skillet with the avocado oil and warm it over high heat. Add the garlic, broccoli, and eggplant and cook, stirring frequently, until the broccoli has softened and the eggplant has collapsed, about 8 minutes.

2   Season the rib eye with salt and add it to the pan. Cook, stirring frequently, until it has the desired level of doneness, 3 to 4 minutes for medium-rare.

3   Add the oyster sauce and soy sauce and toss to combine. Garnish the dish with the chile peppers and enjoy.

YIELD: 4 SERVINGS

ACTIVE TIME: 15 MINUTES

TOTAL TIME: 15 MINUTES

BEST BURGERS EVER

INGREDIENTS

1 tablespoon extra-virgin olive oil

1 lb. ground beef (80 percent lean recommended)

1 teaspoon kosher salt

½ teaspoon white pepper

1 egg white

⅓ cup bread crumbs

4 brioche buns

DIRECTIONS

1   Place the olive oil in a medium or large cast-iron skillet and warm it over medium heat.

2   Place the remaining ingredients, except for the brioche buns, in a bowl and stir until well combined. Divide the mixture into four equal parts and form each piece into a patty that is about 1 inch thick.

3   Place the patties in the pan, cover the pan, and cook until browned, about 5 minutes.

4   Flip the burgers over, cover the pan, and cook until the desired level of doneness is achieved, about 5 to 8 minutes.

5   Remove the burgers from the pan and sandwich them between the buns with your favorite condiments and fixings.

YIELD: 4 SERVINGS
ACTIVE TIME: 15 MINUTES
TOTAL TIME: 15 MINUTES

TACOS

INGREDIENTS

1 tablespoon extra-virgin olive oil

1 lb. ground beef

1 tablespoon kosher salt

2 teaspoons cumin

2 teaspoons paprika

1 tablespoon garlic powder

1 teaspoon cayenne pepper

1 teaspoon chili powder

Corn tortillas, for serving

DIRECTIONS

1 Place the olive oil in a large cast-iron skillet and warm it over medium-high heat.

2 Add the ground beef and all of the seasonings. Cook, breaking up the meat with a wooden spoon, until it is browned and cooked through, about 8 minutes.

3 Serve with the corn tortillas and your favorite taco fixings.

TACOS, SEE PAGE 145

YIELD: 4 SERVINGS

ACTIVE TIME: 30 MINUTES

TOTAL TIME: 2 HOURS AND 30 MINUTES

RISI E BISI

INGREDIENTS

2 tablespoons extra-virgin olive oil

6 oz. thinly sliced prosciutto, cut into ¼-inch-wide strips

2 shallots, minced

1 garlic clove, minced

1 cup Arborio rice

½ cup white wine

Chicken stock, warmed, as needed

1 lb. frozen peas

1 cup freshly grated Parmesan cheese

Juice of ½ lemon

Salt and pepper, to taste

Fresh parsley, chopped, for garnish

DIRECTIONS

1 Place the olive oil in a large cast-iron skillet and warm it over medium-high heat. Add the prosciutto and cook, stirring frequently, until it is golden brown and crispy, about 5 minutes. Using a slotted spoon, transfer the prosciutto to a paper towel–lined plate and let it drain.

2 Add the shallots to the skillet and cook, stirring occasionally, until they start to soften, about 3 minutes.

3 Add the garlic and rice and cook, stirring frequently, for 2 minutes.

4 Add the white wine and cook, stirring frequently, until the rice has absorbed the wine.

5 While stirring continually, add the stock ¼ cup at a time, waiting until each addition has been fully absorbed by the rice before adding more. Continue gradually adding stock until the rice is tender, about 15 minutes.

6 Add the frozen peas and cook, stirring frequently, until warmed through, 4 to 5 minutes.

7 Stir in the Parmesan and lemon juice. Season the dish with salt and pepper, garnish with the crispy prosciutto and parsley, and enjoy.

YIELD: 8 SERVINGS
ACTIVE TIME: 40 MINUTES
TOTAL TIME: 3 HOURS

ROPA VIEJA

INGREDIENTS

2 lbs. flank steak

3 bay leaves

3 garlic cloves, sliced thin

2 yellow onions, sliced

4 cups chicken stock

1 red bell pepper, stem and seeds removed, sliced

1 green bell pepper, stem and seeds removed, sliced

¼ cup plus 1 tablespoon avocado oil

1 (28 oz.) can of tomato puree

1½ cups white wine

1 teaspoon cumin

½ teaspoon smoked paprika

1 teaspoon kosher salt, plus more to taste

⅛ teaspoon black pepper

Cooked jasmine rice, for serving

Sliced avocado, for serving

DIRECTIONS

1   Preheat the oven to 325°F. Place the flank steak, 2 of the bay leaves, the garlic, 1½ of the onions, the stock, and peppers in a cast-iron Dutch oven and place it in the oven. Braise until the meat is tender and easy to shred with a fork, 2 to 2½ hours.

2   Remove the pot from the oven and shred the beef with a fork. Set the mixture aside.

3   Place ¼ cup of the avocado oil in a large cast-iron skillet and warm it over high heat. Add the remaining onion and cook, stirring occasionally, until the onion is translucent, about 3 minutes. Stir in the tomato puree, wine, cumin, paprika, salt, and pepper. Cover the pan, reduce the heat to medium, and cook until the sauce has thickened, about 15 minutes.

4   Stir the shredded meat mixture and remaining bay leaf into the sauce, cover the pan, and cook for 5 minutes.

5   Taste, adjust the seasoning as necessary, and serve with rice and avocado.

ROPA VIEJA, SEE PAGE 149

YIELD: 6 SERVINGS
ACTIVE TIME: 25 MINUTES
TOTAL TIME: 40 MINUTES

CHICKEN TAGINE

INGREDIENTS

2 tablespoons extra-virgin olive oil

8 bone-in, skin-on chicken drumsticks or thighs

Salt and pepper, to taste

1 onion, minced

4 garlic cloves, minced

1 teaspoon grated fresh ginger

Zest of 1 lemon

1 teaspoon paprika

½ teaspoon cumin

⅛ teaspoon cayenne pepper

½ teaspoon coriander

¼ teaspoon cinnamon

½ cup white wine

2 cups chicken stock

1 carrot, peeled and cut into thin half-moons

1 tablespoon honey

¾ cup halved dried apricots

1 (14 oz.) can of chickpeas, drained and rinsed

Fresh mint, chopped, for garnish

Pearl couscous, cooked, for serving

DIRECTIONS

1   Place the olive oil in a cast-iron Dutch oven and warm it over medium-high heat. Season the chicken with salt and pepper, add it to the pot, and cook, stirring occasionally, until it has browned, about 6 minutes. Remove the chicken from the pot and set it aside.

2   Reduce the heat to medium, add the onion, and cook, stirring occasionally, until it has softened, about 5 minutes. Add the garlic, ginger, lemon zest, paprika, cumin, cayenne, coriander, and cinnamon and cook, stirring continually, for 1 minute.

3   Add the white wine and cook until the alcohol has been cooked off, about 3 minutes, scraping up any browned bits from the bottom of the pot.

4   Add the stock, carrot, honey, and apricots and bring the mixture to a simmer. Nestle the chicken into the mixture and cook until it is cooked through (internal temperature of 165°F), about 10 minutes.

5   Add the chickpeas, cover the pot, and cook until they are heated through, about 5 minutes.

6   Garnish the tagine with mint and serve it with couscous.

YIELD: 4 SERVINGS

ACTIVE TIME: 30 MINUTES

TOTAL TIME: 1 HOUR

SHAKSHUKA

INGREDIENTS

2 tablespoons extra-virgin olive oil

1 onion, chopped

2 green bell peppers, stems and seeds removed, chopped

2 garlic cloves, minced

1 teaspoon coriander

1 teaspoon sweet paprika

½ teaspoon cumin

1 teaspoon turmeric

Pinch of red pepper flakes

2 tablespoons tomato paste

5 ripe tomatoes, chopped

Salt and pepper, to taste

6 eggs

1 cup crumbled feta cheese

¼ cup chopped fresh parsley, for garnish

¼ cup chopped fresh mint, for garnish

DIRECTIONS

1   Preheat the oven to 400°F. Place the olive oil in a large cast-iron skillet and warm it over medium heat. Add the onion and cook, stirring occasionally, until it has softened, about 5 minutes. Add the bell peppers and cook, stirring occasionally, until they have softened, about 5 minutes.

2   Add the garlic, coriander, paprika, cumin, turmeric, red pepper flakes, and tomato paste and cook, stirring continually, for 1 minute. Add the tomatoes and bring the mixture to a boil. Reduce the heat, cover the pan, and simmer for 15 minutes.

3   Remove the cover and cook until the shakshuka has reduced slightly, about 5 minutes.

4   Season the shakshuka with salt and pepper. Using the back of a wooden spoon, make six wells in the mixture. Crack an egg into each well and sprinkle the feta over the dish.

5   Place the pan in the oven and cook the shakshuka until the egg whites are set, 6 to 8 minutes. If you prefer to keep the skillet on the stove, cover it and cook until the egg whites are set.

6   Remove the pan from the oven (or remove the cover), garnish the shakshuka with parsley and mint, and enjoy.

YIELD: 6 SERVINGS
ACTIVE TIME: 30 MINUTES
TOTAL TIME: 1 HOUR

RATATOUILLE WITH POACHED EGGS

INGREDIENTS

¼ cup extra-virgin olive oil

1 cup chopped onion

4 garlic cloves, minced

2 tablespoons tomato paste

1 cup chopped red bell pepper

1 cup chopped yellow
bell pepper

1 cup chopped zucchini

2 tablespoons herbes
de Provence

Salt and pepper, to taste

6 eggs

¼ cup fresh basil leaves,
chopped, for garnish

½ cup shaved Parmesan
cheese, for garnish

DIRECTIONS

1   Place the olive oil in a large cast-iron skillet and warm it over medium heat. Add the onion and cook, stirring occasionally, until it has softened, about 5 minutes. Add the garlic and tomato paste and cook, stirring continually, for 1 minute.

2   Add the bell peppers and cook, stirring occasionally, until they have softened, about 5 minutes.

3   Add the zucchini, ½ cup water, and herbes de Provence, cover the pan, and cook for 10 minutes. Remove the cover and cook until the liquid has reduced, about 5 minutes.

4   Season the ratatouille with salt and pepper. Using the back of a wooden spoon, make six wells in the ratatouille. Gently crack an egg into each well, reduce the heat so that the ratatouille simmers, and cover the pan. Cook until the egg whites are set, 6 to 8 minutes.

5   Spoon the ratatouille and poached eggs into bowls, garnish each portion with basil and Parmesan, and enjoy.

YIELD: 4 TO 6 SERVINGS

ACTIVE TIME: 30 MINUTES

TOTAL TIME: 1 HOUR AND 30 MINUTES

EASY PAELLA

INGREDIENTS

2 tablespoons extra-virgin olive oil

1½ lbs. boneless, skinless chicken thighs, chopped into 1-inch cubes

9 oz. ground chorizo

1 onion, chopped

1 red bell pepper, stem and seeds removed, chopped

6 garlic cloves, minced

1 (14 oz.) can of diced tomatoes, drained

2 cups bomba rice

4 cups chicken stock

⅓ cup white wine

½ teaspoon saffron

1 teaspoon paprika

2 bay leaves

Salt and pepper, to taste

16 mussels, scrubbed and debearded

1 lb. jumbo shrimp, shells removed, deveined

Fresh parsley, chopped, for garnish

Lemon wedges, for serving

DIRECTIONS

1   Preheat the oven to 350°F. Place the olive oil in a cast-iron Dutch oven and warm it over medium-high heat. Add the chicken and cook until browned all over, about 6 minutes, stirring as necessary. Remove the chicken with a slotted spoon and place it in a bowl.

2   Add the chorizo to the pot and cook, stirring occasionally, until it is browned all over, about 6 minutes, breaking it up with a wooden spoon as it cooks. Transfer the chorizo to the bowl with the chicken.

3   Add the onion to the pot and cook, stirring occasionally, until it has softened, about 5 minutes. Add the bell pepper and cook, stirring occasionally, for 3 minutes.

4   Add the garlic and cook, stirring frequently, for 1 minute. Stir in the tomatoes and cook until the mixture thickens slightly, about 3 minutes. Add the rice and cook for 2 minutes.

5   Stir in the stock, wine, saffron, paprika, and bay leaves and bring the mixture to a boil, stirring frequently. Return the chicken and chorizo to the pot, season the mixture with salt and pepper, cover the pot, and place it in the oven. Bake until all the liquid has evaporated, about 15 minutes, stirring occasionally.

6   Remove the pot from the oven and place the mussels and shrimp on top of the rice. Make sure to put the mussels in with their hinges facing down. Cover the pot and return it to the oven. Bake until the shrimp are cooked through and the majority of the mussels have opened, about 10 minutes.

7   Remove the paella from the oven and discard the bay leaves and any mussels that did not open. Garnish the paella with parsley and serve with lemon wedges.

YIELD: 6 SERVINGS
ACTIVE TIME: 15 MINUTES
TOTAL TIME: 45 MINUTES

CAPRESE CHICKEN

INGREDIENTS

1 garlic clove, minced

1 teaspoon dried oregano

1 teaspoon garlic powder

Salt and pepper, to taste

2 tablespoons extra-virgin
olive oil

2 lbs. boneless, skinless
chicken breasts, halved along
their equators

1 lb. tomatoes, sliced

1 lb. fresh mozzarella cheese,
drained and sliced

Leaves from 1 bunch of
fresh basil

Balsamic vinegar, for garnish

DIRECTIONS

1   Preheat the oven to 375°F. Place the minced garlic, oregano,
    garlic powder, salt, and pepper in a bowl and stir to combine.
    Place 1 tablespoon of the olive oil and the sliced chicken breasts
    in a bowl and toss to coat. Dredge the chicken breasts in the
    garlic-and-spice mixture and set them aside.

2   Coat the bottom of a large cast-iron skillet with the remaining oil
    and warm it over medium-high heat. Working in batches, sear the
    chicken breasts for 1 minute on each side.

3   When all of the chicken has been seared, place half of the breasts
    in an even layer on the bottom of the skillet. Top with two-thirds
    of the tomatoes and mozzarella, and half of the basil leaves. Place
    the remaining chicken breasts on top in an even layer and cover
    this layer of chicken with the remaining tomatoes, mozzarella,
    and basil.

4   Place the skillet in the oven and cook until the interior temperature
    of the chicken breasts is 165°F, about 10 minutes.

5   Remove the skillet from the oven and let cool for 10 minutes.
    Drizzle the balsamic vinegar over the dish and serve.

YIELD: 6 SERVINGS

ACTIVE TIME: 45 MINUTES

TOTAL TIME: 5 HOURS

CHICKEN FAJITAS

DIRECTIONS

1 To begin preparations for the chicken, place the orange juice, lime juice, garlic, jalapeño, cilantro, cumin, oregano, salt, and pepper in a bowl and stir to combine. Stir in the olive oil, add the chicken, and stir until it is evenly coated. Cover the bowl with plastic wrap and chill it in the refrigerator for 4 hours.

2 Remove the chicken from the refrigerator and let it come to room temperature.

3 Warm a large cast-iron skillet over medium-high heat. Add the chicken and cook, turning it as necessary, until it is browned and cooked through, about 8 minutes. Transfer the chicken to a plate and tent with aluminum foil to keep warm.

4 To prepare the vegetables, reduce the heat to medium, add the olive oil to the skillet, and then add the onion, bell peppers, and garlic. Cook, stirring frequently, until the vegetables start to soften, about 5 minutes. Stir in the lime juice and cilantro, season the mixture with salt and pepper, and cook until the vegetables are tender, about 10 minutes.

5 Push the vegetables to one side of the pan and place the chicken on the other side. Serve immediately with tortillas and Pico de Gallo.

INGREDIENTS

For the Chicken

½ cup orange juice

Juice of 1 lime

4 garlic cloves, minced

1 jalapeño chile pepper, stem and seeds removed, diced

2 tablespoons chopped fresh cilantro

1 teaspoon cumin

1 teaspoon dried oregano

Salt and pepper, to taste

3 tablespoons extra-virgin olive oil

4 boneless, skinless chicken breasts, sliced into thin strips

For the Vegetables

2 tablespoons extra-virgin olive oil

1 red onion, sliced thin

3 bell peppers, stems and seeds removed, sliced thin

2 jalapeño chile peppers, stems and seeds removed, sliced thin

3 garlic cloves, minced

¼ cup fresh lime juice

½ cup fresh cilantro, chopped

Salt and pepper, to taste

Flour or corn tortillas, for serving

Pico de Gallo (see sidebar), for serving

PICO DE GALLO

Place 4 diced plum tomatoes, 1 diced jalapeño pepper, ½ cup chopped red onion, ¼ cup finely chopped fresh cilantro, and the zest and juice of ½ lime in a mixing bowl and stir to combine. Season with salt to taste and refrigerate for 1 hour before serving.

CHICKEN CURRY

INGREDIENTS

5 tablespoons green curry paste

6 boneless, skinless
chicken thighs

2 yellow onions, sliced

2 red bell peppers, stems and
seeds removed, sliced

3-inch piece of fresh ginger,
peeled and mashed

1 garlic clove, mashed

1 tablespoon fish sauce

1 tablespoon Madras
curry powder

1 (14 oz.) can of coconut milk

2 tablespoons chopped fresh
Thai basil, plus more for garnish

1½ cups basmati rice

Fresh cilantro, chopped,
for garnish

Lime wedges, for serving

DIRECTIONS

1   Preheat the oven to 375°F. Rub 2 tablespoons of the green
curry paste on the chicken and let it rest at room temperature
for 30 minutes.

2   Place a large cast-iron skillet over medium-high heat and add
the chicken. Cook until it is browned, turn the chicken over, and
cook for another 3 minutes, until it is browned on the other side.
Remove the chicken from the skillet and set it aside.

3   Add the onions, peppers, ginger, and garlic to the skillet and cook,
stirring frequently and scraping to remove any browned bits from
the bottom the pan, until the vegetables are tender, 5 to 7 minutes.

4   Stir in the remaining green curry paste and cook, stirring
occasionally, until fragrant, about 2 minutes.

5   Stir in the fish sauce, curry powder, coconut milk, and Thai basil.
Add the rice and 1 cup water, stir until incorporated, and then
return the chicken to the pan. Cover the skillet and place it in
the oven.

6   Bake until the rice is tender and has absorbed all of the liquid,
about 25 minutes. Remove the pan from the oven, taste the curry,
and adjust the seasoning as necessary. Garnish with cilantro and
additional Thai basil and serve with the lime wedges.

YIELD: 6 SERVINGS
ACTIVE TIME: 30 MINUTES
TOTAL TIME: 2 HOURS AND 30 MINUTES

GOULASH

INGREDIENTS

2 tablespoons extra-virgin olive oil

3 lbs. beef chuck, trimmed

3 yellow onions, chopped

2 carrots, peeled and chopped

2 bell peppers, stems and seeds removed, chopped

1 teaspoon caraway seeds

¼ cup all-purpose flour

3 tablespoons sweet Hungarian paprika

3 tablespoons tomato paste

2 garlic cloves, minced

1 teaspoon sugar

Salt and pepper, to taste

2 cups beef stock

1 lb. wide egg noodles

1 cup sour cream

DIRECTIONS

1   Place the olive oil in a cast-iron Dutch oven and warm it over medium heat. Working in batches to avoid crowding the pot, add the meat and cook until it is browned all over, turning it as necessary. Remove the browned beef from the pot and set it aside.

2   Reduce the heat to medium-low. Let the pot cool for 2 minutes and then add the onions, carrots, and bell peppers. Stir to coat with the pan drippings and cook the vegetables, stirring occasionally, until they are brown, about 10 minutes.

3   Stir in the caraway seeds and cook until they are fragrant, about 1 minute.

4   Stir in the flour, paprika, tomato paste, garlic, sugar, salt, and pepper, add the stock, and use a wooden spoon to scrape up any browned bits from the bottom of the pan.

5   Bring the goulash to a boil, reduce the heat, and let it simmer until it thickens slightly, about 10 minutes. Return the meat to the Dutch oven, cover the pot, and simmer the goulash over low heat until the meat is very tender, about 2 hours.

6   Approximately 20 minutes before the goulash will be done, bring water to a boil in a large pot. Add salt and the egg noodles to the boiling water and cook until al dente. Drain and set aside.

7   To serve, stir the sour cream into the goulash and then ladle it over the cooked egg noodles.

YIELD: 4 SERVINGS
ACTIVE TIME: 20 MINUTES
TOTAL TIME: 1 HOUR AND 45 MINUTES

DAL

INGREDIENTS

2 tablespoons extra-virgin olive oil

1 yellow onion, chopped

2 garlic cloves, minced

2 teaspoons red pepper flakes

2 curry leaves (optional)

1 teaspoon kosher salt

1½ cups yellow split peas, picked over and rinsed

1 teaspoon turmeric

1 cup fresh peas

DIRECTIONS

1 Place the olive oil in a cast-iron Dutch oven and warm it over medium-high heat. Add the onion, garlic, red pepper flakes, curry leaves (if using), and salt and cook, stirring continually, until the onion is translucent, about 3 minutes.

2 Add the split peas, 4 cups water, and turmeric and bring the mixture to a simmer. Cover the pot and gently simmer for 1 hour, stirring two or three times.

3 Remove the lid and simmer, stirring occasionally, until the dal has thickened, about 30 minutes.

4 When the dal has the consistency of porridge, stir in the fresh peas and cook until they are warmed through. Ladle the dal into warmed bowls and enjoy.

SHRIMP & GRITS

INGREDIENTS

1 cup quick-cooking grits

2 large eggs

5 tablespoons unsalted butter, at room temperature

¾ cup milk

Salt and pepper, to taste

1 lb. cheddar cheese, grated

1 tablespoon extra-virgin olive oil

1 lb. shrimp, shells removed, deveined

2 garlic cloves, minced

1 tablespoon fresh lemon juice

2 dashes of Tabasco

DIRECTIONS

1 Preheat the oven to 425°F. Place 4 cups water in a large cast-iron skillet and bring it to a boil. While stirring constantly, slowly pour in the grits. Cover the pan, reduce the heat to low, and cook, while stirring occasionally, until the grits are quite thick, about 5 minutes. Remove from heat.

2 Place the eggs, 4 tablespoons of the butter, and milk in a bowl, season the mixture with salt and pepper, and stir to combine. Stir the cooked grits into the egg mixture, add three-quarters of the cheese, and stir to incorporate.

3 Wipe out the skillet, coat it with the remaining butter, and pour the grits mixture into the skillet. Place the skillet in the oven and bake for 30 minutes. Remove, sprinkle the remaining cheese on top, and return the grits to the oven. Bake until the cheese is melted and the grits are firm, about 15 minutes. Remove the grits from the oven and let them cool for 10 minutes.

4 Place the olive oil in a medium cast-iron skillet and warm it over medium-high heat. Add the shrimp to the skillet, season them with salt and pepper, and cook for 1 minute. Turn the shrimp over, stir in the garlic, lemon juice, and Tabasco, and cook until the shrimp are pink and opaque throughout, 1 to 2 minutes.

5 Divide the grits among four bowls, place a few shrimp on top of each portion, and enjoy.

YIELD: 4 SERVINGS
ACTIVE TIME: 15 MINUTES
TOTAL TIME: 25 MINUTES

CHICKEN PANINI WITH SUN-DRIED TOMATO AIOLI

INGREDIENTS

For the Aioli

1 cup chopped sun-dried tomatoes

1 cup mayonnaise

1 tablespoon whole grain mustard

2 tablespoons finely chopped fresh parsley

2 tablespoons minced scallions

1 teaspoon white balsamic vinegar

1 garlic clove, minced

2 teaspoons kosher salt

1 teaspoon black pepper

For the Sandwiches

8 slices of crusty bread

8 slices of cheddar cheese

2 leftover chicken breasts, sliced

12 slices of cooked bacon

1 cup arugula

1 tablespoon extra-virgin olive oil

DIRECTIONS

1   Preheat the oven to 450°F and place a small cast-iron skillet in the oven as it warms. As the skillet is warming up, prepare the aioli. Place all of the ingredients in a mixing bowl and stir until combined. Set the aioli aside.

2   To begin preparations for the sandwiches, spread some of the aioli on each slice of bread. Place a slice of cheddar on each slice of bread. Divide the chicken among 4 pieces of the bread. Top each portion of chicken with 3 slices of bacon and ¼ cup of the arugula and assemble the sandwiches.

3   When the small skillet in the oven is hot, place the olive oil in a large cast-iron skillet and warm it over medium heat. Place a sandwich in the large cast-iron skillet, place the small skillet on top of the sandwich, and cook it between the two pans until the cheese has melted and there is a nice crust on the bread. Repeat with the remaining sandwiches and enjoy.

YIELD: 4 TO 6 SERVINGS

ACTIVE TIME: 15 MINUTES

TOTAL TIME: 15 MINUTES

CLAMS WITH CHORIZO

INGREDIENTS

24 littleneck clams, scrubbed well and rinsed

1 tablespoon extra-virgin olive oil

1 yellow onion, chopped

3 garlic cloves, minced

2 cups cherry tomatoes

2 oz. Spanish chorizo, minced

2 tablespoons unsalted butter, chopped

DIRECTIONS

1   Pick over the clams and discard any that are open, cracked, or damaged.

2   Place the olive oil in a large cast-iron skillet and warm it over medium heat. Add the onion and cook, without stirring, for 2 minutes. Add the garlic and tomatoes and cook, stirring occasionally, until the tomatoes start to collapse, about 6 minutes.

3   Add the chorizo, stir to incorporate, and cook for 5 minutes. Add the clams, cover the pan, and cook until the majority of the clams have opened, about 2 minutes.

4   Discard any clams that did not open. Add the butter to the pan, stir until it has melted, and enjoy.

YIELD: 4 SERVINGS
ACTIVE TIME: 15 MINUTES
TOTAL TIME: 15 MINUTES

THAI BASIL CHICKEN

INGREDIENTS

¼ cup fish sauce

¼ cup soy sauce

2 tablespoons brown sugar

4 boneless, skinless chicken breasts, diced

2 tablespoons avocado oil

3 shallots, sliced thin

2 red bell peppers, stems and seeds removed, sliced thin

2 fresh red bird's eye chili peppers, stems and seeds removed, sliced thin

3 garlic cloves, chopped

1½ cups fresh Thai basil

DIRECTIONS

1 Place the fish sauce, soy sauce, 2 tablespoons water, and sugar in a bowl and stir to combine. Set half of the marinade aside, add the chicken to the bowl, and let the chicken marinate.

2 Place the avocado oil in a large cast-iron skillet and warm it over medium-high heat. Add the shallots, bell peppers, chilies, and garlic and cook, stirring continually, for 2 minutes.

3 Remove the chicken from the marinade and add the chicken to the pan. Cook, stirring frequently, until it is almost cooked through, about 6 minutes.

4 Add the reserved marinade and cook for another 1 or 2 minutes, until the chicken is cooked through.

5 Remove the pan from heat and stir in 1 cup of the basil. Serve immediately, topping each portion with some of the remaining Thai basil leaves.

YIELD: 2 SERVINGS

ACTIVE TIME: 6 MINUTES

TOTAL TIME: 15 MINUTES

FILET MIGNON WITH PEPPERCORN CREAM SAUCE

INGREDIENTS

2 tablespoons canola oil

2 tablespoons peppercorns

1 cup heavy cream

Salt, to taste

1 lb. filet mignon

2 tablespoons unsalted butter

Fresh rosemary, chopped, for garnish

DIRECTIONS

1   Place the canola oil in a large cast-iron skillet and warm it over high heat.

2   Using a mortar and pestle or a spice grinder, roughly grind the peppercorns. Place them in a separate large skillet and toast for 1 minute. Add the cream and a pinch of salt, reduce the heat to medium-low, and cook, stirring constantly, for 2 minutes. Remove the pan from heat and set it aside.

3   Season the filet mignon with salt, place them in the cast-iron skillet, and cook until they are well seared on one side, about 4 minutes.

4   Flip the steaks over, add the butter to the pan, tilt the pan slightly, and spoon the butter-and-oil mixture over the top of the steaks. Cook the steaks until they reach the desired level of doneness, 3 to 4 minutes.

5   Transfer the steaks to a plate, spoon the cream sauce over the top, garnish them with rosemary, and enjoy.

YIELD: 4 SERVINGS
ACTIVE TIME: 15 MINUTES
TOTAL TIME: 15 MINUTES

PORK MILANESA

INGREDIENTS

2 cups fine bread crumbs

4 large eggs

1 cup extra-virgin olive oil

2 lbs. pork cutlets (¼ inch thick)

Salt, to taste

DIRECTIONS

1   Place the bread crumbs in a shallow bowl. Place the eggs in a separate bowl and beat until they are scrambled.

2   Place the olive oil in a large cast-iron skillet and warm it over medium-high heat until it is hot enough that a bread crumb sizzles gently when added.

3   Season the pork cutlets with salt, dredge them in the beaten eggs, and then in the bread crumbs until they are coated all over. Gently press down on the bread crumbs so that they adhere to the pork.

4   Slip the cutlets into the hot oil and fry until golden brown on both sides and cooked through, 8 to 10 minutes. Transfer the milanesa to a paper towel–lined plate to drain and enjoy.

YIELD: 4 SERVINGS
ACTIVE TIME: 15 MINUTES
TOTAL TIME: 25 MINUTES

CHICKEN DE CHAMPIÑONES

INGREDIENTS

2 tablespoons extra-virgin olive oil

1½ lbs. chicken cutlets

Salt and pepper, to taste

6 button mushrooms, sliced

1 shallot, chopped

1 garlic clove, sliced

¼ cup white wine

¼ cup heavy cream

¼ cup shredded Oaxaca cheese

1 teaspoon cumin

Fresh cilantro, chopped, for garnish

DIRECTIONS

1   Place the olive oil in a large cast-iron skillet and warm it over medium-high heat. Season the chicken with salt and pepper, place it in the pan, and sear for 1 minute on each side.

2   Add the mushrooms and cook for about 30 seconds. Add the shallot and garlic and cook for another 30 seconds, stirring frequently.

3   Deglaze the pan with the white wine and cook until the liquid has reduced by half, about 5 minutes. Stir in the heavy cream, Oaxaca cheese, and cumin and cook until the cheese has melted and the chicken is cooked through, about 6 minutes.

4   Garnish the dish with cilantro and enjoy.

YIELD: 2 SERVINGS
ACTIVE TIME: 15 MINUTES
TOTAL TIME: 15 MINUTES

PAN-SEARED STRIP STEAK

INGREDIENTS

1 lb. New York strip steak

2 teaspoons kosher salt

2 tablespoons canola oil

4 tablespoons unsalted butter

2 sprigs of fresh rosemary

DIRECTIONS

1 Pat the steak dry and season both sides of the steak with salt.

2 Place the canola oil in a large cast-iron skillet and warm it over medium-high heat. Place the steak in the pan and cook it until the bottom side has a nice sear on it, 4 to 5 minutes.

3 Flip the steak over, add 2 tablespoons of butter to the pan, tilt the pan slightly, and spoon the butter and pan juices over the top of the steak.

4 Cook the steak for another 3 to 4 minutes, or until the desired doneness is achieved. Just before removing the steak from the pan, add the remaining butter and rosemary, tilt the pan slightly, and spoon the butter and pan juices over the steak. Remove the steak from the pan and let it rest on a cutting board for 2 minutes before serving.

YIELD: 4 SERVINGS

ACTIVE TIME: 10 MINUTES

TOTAL TIME: 45 MINUTES

ROASTED GRAPES & SAUSAGE

INGREDIENTS

½ lb. sausage (Hungarian or spicy Italian recommended)

1 bunch of green or red grapes

3 oz. fresh mozzarella cheese, torn

2 tablespoons balsamic vinegar

DIRECTIONS

1 Preheat the oven to 500°F. Cut the sausage into ¼-inch-thick slices, place them in a large cast-iron skillet, and add the grapes. Toss to evenly distribute.

2 Place the skillet in the oven and cook until the sausage is well browned and cooked through and the grapes have collapsed, 15 to 20 minutes.

3 Remove the skillet from the oven and transfer the mixture to a serving platter.

4 Sprinkle the mozzarella over the sausage and grapes, drizzle the balsamic vinegar over the dish, and enjoy.

LAMB SHARBA

INGREDIENTS

2 tablespoons extra-virgin olive oil

¾ lb. boneless leg of lamb, cut into 1-inch cubes

1 onion, chopped

1 tomato, quartered, seeds removed, sliced thin

1 garlic clove, minced

1 tablespoon tomato paste

1 bunch of fresh mint, sprigs tied together with twine, plus more for garnish

2 cinnamon sticks

1¼ teaspoons turmeric

1¼ teaspoons paprika

½ teaspoon cumin

8 cups chicken stock

1 (14 oz.) can of chickpeas, drained and rinsed

¾ cup orzo

Salt and pepper, to taste

DIRECTIONS

1 Place half of the olive oil in a cast-iron Dutch oven and warm it over medium-high heat. Add the lamb and cook, turning it as necessary, until it is browned all over, about 5 minutes. Remove the lamb with a slotted spoon and place it on a paper towel–lined plate.

2 Add the onion to the pot and cook, stirring occasionally, until it starts to soften, about 5 minutes. Add the tomato, garlic, tomato paste, mint, cinnamon sticks, turmeric, paprika, and cumin and cook, stirring continually, for 1 minute.

3 Add the stock and bring the mixture to a boil. Return the seared lamb to the pot, reduce the heat, and simmer until the lamb is tender, about 30 minutes.

4 Add the chickpeas and orzo and cook until the orzo is tender, about 10 minutes.

5 Remove the mint and discard it. Season the soup with salt and pepper and ladle it into warmed bowls. Garnish with additional mint and enjoy.

DESSERTS

As you've likely come to expect, cast iron does not beg off when called upon to soothe a sweet tooth. In fact, a medium cast-iron skillet just may be the world's very best pie plate, guaranteeing the crust is light, crispy, and evenly cooked, and adding yet another layer of appealing aesthetics with its dark, handsome gleam. Whatever one craves at the end of a long day—pie, fresh fruit swaddled in a decadent custard, a moist slice of cake, airy pastry, even cookies—cast iron is here to make sure your needs are met.

YIELD: 2 (9-INCH) PIECRUSTS
ACTIVE TIME: 15 MINUTES
TOTAL TIME: 2 HOURS AND 15 MINUTES

PERFECT PIECRUSTS

INGREDIENTS

1 cup unsalted butter, cubed

2½ cups all-purpose flour, plus more as needed

½ teaspoon kosher salt

4 teaspoons sugar

½ cup ice water

DIRECTIONS

1 Transfer the butter to a small bowl and place it in the freezer.

2 Place the flour, salt, and sugar in a food processor and pulse a few times until combined.

3 Add the chilled butter and pulse until the mixture is crumbly, consisting of pea-sized clumps.

4 Add the water and pulse until the mixture comes together as a dough.

5 Place the dough on a flour-dusted work surface and fold it over itself until it is a ball. Divide the dough in two and flatten each piece into a 1-inch-thick disk. Cover each piece completely with plastic wrap and place the dough in the refrigerator for at least 2 hours before rolling it out to fit your skillet.

YIELD: 1 (9-INCH) PIECRUST

ACTIVE TIME: 10 MINUTES

TOTAL TIME: 1 HOUR

GRAHAM CRACKER PIECRUST

INGREDIENTS

1½ cups graham cracker crumbs

2 tablespoons sugar

1 tablespoon pure maple syrup

6 tablespoons unsalted butter, melted

DIRECTIONS

1   Preheat the oven to 375°F. Place the graham cracker crumbs and sugar in a large mixing bowl and stir to combine. Add the maple syrup and 5 tablespoons of the melted butter and stir until thoroughly combined.

2   Coat a 9-inch cast-iron skillet with the remaining butter. Pour the graham cracker mixture into the pan and gently press it into shape. Line the crust with aluminum paper, fill it with uncooked rice, dried beans, or pie weights, and place the pan in the oven. Bake for about 10 minutes, until the crust is firm.

3   Remove the pan from the oven, discard the aluminum foil and weights, and allow the crust to cool completely before filling.

PERFECT PIECRUSTS, SEE PAGE 192

PLUM GALETTE

INGREDIENTS

1 ball of Perfect Piecrust dough (see page 192)

All-purpose flour, as needed

5 plums, pits removed, sliced

½ cup plus 1 tablespoon sugar

Juice of ½ lemon

3 tablespoons cornstarch

Pinch of fine sea salt

2 tablespoons blackberry jam

1 egg, beaten

DIRECTIONS

1   Preheat the oven to 400°F. Coat a medium cast-iron skillet with nonstick cooking spray. Place the ball of dough on a flour-dusted work surface, roll it out to 9 inches, and place it in the skillet.

2   Place the plums, the ½ cup of sugar, lemon juice, cornstarch, and salt in a mixing bowl and stir until the plums are evenly coated.

3   Spread the jam over the crust, making sure to leave a 1-inch border around the edge. Distribute the plum mixture on top of the jam and fold the crust over it. Brush the folded-over crust with the beaten egg and sprinkle the remaining sugar over it.

4   Place the galette in the oven and bake until the crust is golden brown and the filling is bubbly, about 35 to 40 minutes.

5   Remove the galette from the oven and allow it to cool before serving.

YIELD: 1 PIE
ACTIVE TIME: 25 MINUTES
TOTAL TIME: 1 HOUR AND 15 MINUTES

MIXED BERRY PIE

INGREDIENTS

Unsalted butter, as needed

1½ cups fresh blueberries

1 cup fresh blackberries

1 cup fresh raspberries

1½ cups fresh strawberries, hulled and halved

1 tablespoon fresh lemon juice

½ cup light brown sugar

2 tablespoons cornstarch

½ cup unsweetened raspberry preserves

2 Perfect Piecrusts (see page 192), rolled out

1 egg, beaten

DIRECTIONS

1   Preheat the oven to 375°F and coat a 9-inch cast-iron skillet with butter or nonstick cooking spray.

2   Place the berries, lemon juice, brown sugar, and cornstarch in a large bowl and toss to combine. Transfer the fruit to a large saucepan and cook over medium heat until the berries start to collapse, 7 to 10 minutes. Stir in the preserves, remove the pan from heat, and set the mixture aside.

3   Place one of the crusts in the skillet, trim away any excess, and fill the crust with the berry mixture.

4   Cut the other crust into 1-inch-wide strips. Lay some of the strips over the pie and trim the strips so that they fit. To make a lattice crust, lift every other strip and fold them back so you can place another strip across those strips that remain flat. Lay the folded strips back down over the cross-strip. Fold back the strips that you laid the cross-strip on top of and repeat until the lattice covers the surface of the pie. Brush the strips with the beaten egg, taking care not to get any egg on the filling.

5   Place the pie in the oven and bake for 45 minutes, until the crust is golden brown and the filling is bubbly.

6   Remove the pie from the oven and let it cool before enjoying.

YIELD: 1 PIE

ACTIVE TIME: 20 MINUTES

TOTAL TIME: 4 HOURS AND 30 MINUTES

SWEET POTATO PIE

INGREDIENTS

15 oz. sweet potato puree

2 eggs

½ cup heavy cream

1 cup dark brown sugar

1 teaspoon cinnamon

½ teaspoon freshly grated nutmeg

¼ teaspoon ground ginger

½ teaspoon pure vanilla extract

¼ teaspoon kosher salt

1 Graham Cracker Piecrust (see page 193)

Whipped cream, for serving

DIRECTIONS

1 Preheat the oven to 350°F. Place the sweet potato puree, eggs, heavy cream, brown sugar, cinnamon, nutmeg, ginger, vanilla, and salt in a mixing bowl and whisk until smooth.

2 Pour the filling into the baked crust, place the pie in the oven, and bake until the filling is just set, about 30 minutes.

3 Remove the pie from the oven, place it on a cooling rack, and let it sit at room temperature for 30 minutes.

4 Place the pie in the refrigerator and chill it for 3 hours.

5 To serve, top each slice with a dollop of whipped cream.

APPLE PIE

INGREDIENTS

2 Perfect Piecrusts (see page 192), rolled out

3 Honeycrisp apples, peeled, cores removed, sliced

3 Granny Smith apples, peeled, cores removed, sliced

½ cup sugar

¼ cup light brown sugar

1½ tablespoons cornstarch

1 teaspoon cinnamon

½ teaspoon freshly grated nutmeg

¼ teaspoon cardamom

Zest and juice of 1 lemon

¼ teaspoon fine sea salt

1 egg, beaten

Sanding sugar, for topping

DIRECTIONS

1   Preheat the oven to 375°F. Coat a 9-inch cast-iron skillet with nonstick cooking spray, place one of the rolled-out crusts in it, and trim away any excess.

2   Place the apples, sugar, brown sugar, cornstarch, cinnamon, nutmeg, cardamom, lemon zest, lemon juice, and salt in a mixing bowl and toss until the apples are evenly coated.

3   Fill the crust in the skillet with the apple filling, lay the other crust over the top, and crimp the edge to seal. Brush the top crust with the egg and sprinkle the sanding sugar over it. Cut several slits in the top crust.

4   Place the pie in the oven and bake until the crust is golden brown and the filling is bubbly and has thickened, about 50 minutes.

5   Remove the pie from the oven and let it cool completely before serving.

YIELD: 1 TART

ACTIVE TIME: 1 HOUR

TOTAL TIME: 50 HOURS

TARTE TATIN

INGREDIENTS

6 to 8 Honeycrisp apples, peeled, cores removed, quartered

1⅓ cups all-purpose flour, plus more as needed

¼ cup confectioners' sugar

½ teaspoon fine sea salt

½ cup unsalted butter, chilled

1 egg, beaten

6 tablespoons salted butter, softened

⅔ cup sugar

DIRECTIONS

1   Place the apples in a mixing bowl and let them sit in the refrigerator for 48 hours. This will dry the apples out, keeping the amount of liquid in the tarte tatin to a reasonable level.

2   Whisk together the flour, confectioners' sugar, and salt in a large bowl. Add the unsalted butter and use your fingers or a pastry blender to work the mixture until it is a collection of coarse clumps. Add the egg and work the mixture until the dough just holds together. Shape it into a ball and cover it with plastic wrap. Flatten it into a 4-inch disk and refrigerate for 1 hour. If preparing ahead of time, the dough will keep in the refrigerator overnight.

3   Preheat the oven to 375°F. Coat a 10-inch cast-iron skillet with the salted butter and place the pan over low heat. When the butter is melted, remove the skillet from heat and sprinkle the sugar evenly over the butter. Place the apple slices in a circular pattern, starting at the center of the pan and working out to the edge. The pieces should overlap and face the same direction.

4   Place the dough on a flour-dusted work surface and roll it out to ⅛ inch thick. Use the roller to carefully roll up the dough. Place it over the apples and tuck the dough in around the edges.

5   Place the skillet over low heat and gradually raise it until the juices in the pan are a deep amber color, about 7 minutes.

6   Place the skillet in the oven and bake until the crust is golden brown and firm, 35 to 40 minutes.

7   Remove the tart from the oven, let it cool for about 5 minutes, and then run a knife around the edge to loosen the tart. Using oven mitts, carefully invert the tart onto a large plate. Place any apples that are stuck to the skillet back on the tart and enjoy.

YIELD: 1 PIE
ACTIVE TIME: 30 MINUTES
TOTAL TIME: 1 HOUR AND 45 MINUTES

CHERRY PIE

INGREDIENTS

4 cups Rainier cherries, pits removed

2 cups sugar

2 tablespoons fresh lemon juice

3 tablespoons cornstarch

1 tablespoon water

¼ teaspoon almond extract

2 Perfect Piecrusts (see page 192), rolled out

Unsalted butter, as needed

1 egg, beaten

DIRECTIONS

1   Preheat oven to 350°F. Place the cherries, sugar, and lemon juice in a saucepan and cook, stirring occasionally, over medium heat until the mixture is syrupy, 7 to 10 minutes.

2   Combine the cornstarch and water in a small bowl and then stir this mixture into the saucepan. Reduce the heat to low and cook, stirring frequently, until the mixture has thickened. Remove the pan from heat, stir in the almond extract, and let the filling cool.

3   When the cherry mixture has cooled, coat a 9-inch cast-iron skillet with butter or nonstick cooking spray. Place one of the crusts in the pan and trim away any excess. Pour the filling into the crust, top with the other crust, and crimp the edge to seal. Make a few slits in the top crust and brush it with the beaten egg.

4   Place the pie in the oven and bake until the top crust is golden brown and the filling is bubbly, about 45 minutes.

5   Remove the pie from the oven and let it cool before enjoying.

YIELD: 1 PIE

ACTIVE TIME: 15 MINUTES

TOTAL TIME: 2 HOURS

BLUEBERRY PIE

INGREDIENTS

4 cups fresh or frozen blueberries

1 tablespoon fresh lemon juice

1 cup plus 2 tablespoons sugar

3 tablespoons all-purpose flour

½ cup unsalted butter

1 cup packed light brown sugar

2 Perfect Piecrusts (see page 192), rolled out

1 egg white

DIRECTIONS

1   Preheat the oven to 350°F. If using frozen blueberries, it's not necessary to thaw them completely. Place the blueberries, lemon juice, 1 cup of the sugar, and the flour in a mixing bowl and stir to combine.

2   Place a 9-inch cast-iron skillet over medium heat and melt the butter in it. Add the brown sugar and cook, stirring continually, until the brown sugar has dissolved, 1 to 2 minutes. Remove the pan from heat.

3   Gently place one crust over the butter-and-sugar mixture and trim away any excess. Fill the crust with the blueberries, place the other crust on top, and crimp the edge to seal. Brush the top crust with the egg white, cut a few slits in it, and then sprinkle the remaining sugar over the top.

4   Place the pie in the oven and bake until the crust is golden brown and the filling is bubbly, 50 to 60 minutes.

5   Remove the pie from the oven and let it cool before enjoying.

YIELD: 1 CAKE

ACTIVE TIME: 20 MINUTES

TOTAL TIME: 1 HOUR AND 20 MINUTES

SALTED HONEY & APPLE UPSIDE-DOWN CAKE

INGREDIENTS

¾ cup all-purpose flour

1 teaspoon baking powder

¾ teaspoon kosher salt

½ teaspoon cinnamon

¼ cup sour cream, plus more for serving

¼ cup avocado oil

2 teaspoons pure vanilla extract

½ cup sugar

2 eggs

½ tablespoon unsalted butter

¼ cup honey, plus more for serving

1 baking apple, peel and core removed, sliced into thin rounds

Maldon sea salt, for garnish

DIRECTIONS

1   Preheat the oven to 350°F. Place the flour, baking powder, ½ teaspoon of the salt, and the cinnamon in a small bowl and whisk until combined.

2   Place the sour cream, avocado oil, and vanilla in a separate bowl and stir until combined. Place the sugar and eggs in a separate bowl and whisk until the mixture is foamy, about 2 minutes.

3   Add half of the flour mixture to the egg mixture and gently stir to incorporate. Stir in half of the sour cream mixture, add the remaining flour mixture, and stir until incorporated. Add the remaining sour cream mixture and stir until the mixture just comes together. Set the batter aside.

4   Butter the bottom and sides of an 8-inch cast-iron skillet and add the honey, swirling the pan to ensure the honey covers as much of the pan as possible. Sprinkle the remaining salt over the honey.

5   Arrange the apples on top of the honey, overlapping them to fit the pan. Pour the cake batter over the apples and tap the pan on a counter a few times to remove any large bubbles.

6   Place the cake in the oven and bake until it is golden brown and springs back when gently touched with a finger, about 30 minutes.

7   Remove the cake from the oven and let it cool in the pan for 10 minutes. Run an offset spatula or knife around the pan and invert the cake onto a cooling rack. Let the cake cool for another 20 minutes before transferring to a platter and sprinkling the Maldon sea salt over the top. Serve with additional sour cream and honey.

YIELD: 6 SERVINGS

ACTIVE TIME: 15 MINUTES

TOTAL TIME: 40 MINUTES

PEACH COBBLER

INGREDIENTS

5 peaches, pits removed, sliced

¼ cup sugar

All-purpose flour, as needed

Dough from Biscuits (see page 42)

1 teaspoon cinnamon

Vanilla ice cream, for serving

DIRECTIONS

1   Preheat the oven to 400°F and place a medium cast-iron skillet in the oven as it warms.

2   Place the peaches, sugar, and 1 or 2 tablespoons of flour in a bowl and stir to combine. The amount of flour you use will depend on how juicy the peaches are; more juice means more flour is required. Remove the skillet from the oven, transfer the mixture to the pan, and place it in the oven. Bake for 10 minutes.

3   While the peaches are in the oven, place the dough on a flour-dusted work surface, and roll it out until it is a 1-inch-thick rectangle. Use a mason jar or a ring cutter to cut the dough into 3-inch circles.

4   Remove the skillet from the oven and place the biscuits on top of the peaches in an even layer. Sprinkle the cinnamon over the biscuits and return the skillet to the oven. Bake until the biscuits are golden brown and the filling is bubbling, 10 to 12 minutes.

5   Remove the cobbler from the oven, let it cool briefly, and serve with vanilla ice cream.

YIELD: 4 SERVINGS

ACTIVE TIME: 20 MINUTES

TOTAL TIME: 1 HOUR

APPLE DUTCH BABY

INGREDIENTS

4 tablespoons unsalted butter

2 firm and tart apples, cores and peels removed, sliced

¼ cup plus 3 tablespoons sugar

1 tablespoon cinnamon

¾ cup all-purpose flour

¼ teaspoon fine sea salt

¾ cup milk

4 eggs

1 teaspoon pure vanilla extract

Confectioners' sugar, for dusting

DIRECTIONS

1 Preheat the oven to 425°F and position a rack in the middle. Warm a medium cast-iron skillet over medium-high heat. Add the butter and apples to the pan and cook, stirring frequently, until the apples start to soften, 3 to 4 minutes. Add ¼ cup of the sugar and the cinnamon and cook, stirring occasionally, for another 3 to 4 minutes. Distribute the apple mixture evenly over the bottom of the skillet and remove the pan from heat.

2 In a large bowl, combine the remaining sugar, flour, and salt. In a separate bowl, combine the milk, eggs, and vanilla. Add the wet mixture to the dry mixture and stir until it comes together as a smooth batter. Pour the batter over the apples.

3 Place the skillet in the oven and bake until the baby is puffy and golden brown, about 20 minutes. Remove the skillet from the oven and let it cool for a few minutes.

4 Run a knife along the edge of the skillet to loosen the baby, dust it with confectioners' sugar, and serve warm.

APPLE DUTCH BABY, SEE PAGE 213

YIELD: 6 SERVINGS
ACTIVE TIME: 20 MINUTES
TOTAL TIME: 45 MINUTES

CHERRY CLAFOUTIS

INGREDIENTS

½ cup unsalted butter, melted

1 cup plus 2 teaspoons sugar

⅔ cup all-purpose flour

½ teaspoon fine sea salt

1 teaspoon pure vanilla extract

3 eggs, beaten

1 cup milk

3 cups cherries, pits removed

Confectioners' sugar, for topping

DIRECTIONS

1   Preheat the oven to 400°F. Place three-quarters of the butter, ½ cup of the sugar, the flour, salt, vanilla, eggs, and milk in a large mixing bowl and stir until the mixture is well combined and smooth. Set the batter aside.

2   Coat a medium cast-iron skillet with the remaining butter and put the skillet in the oven to warm up.

3   When the skillet is warm, remove it from the oven, place ½ cup of the sugar in the skillet, and shake to distribute it evenly. Distribute the cherries in the skillet and then pour in the batter. Sprinkle the remaining sugar on top, place the skillet in the oven, and bake until the custard is golden brown and set in the middle, about 30 minutes.

4   Remove the clafoutis from the oven, sprinkle confectioners' sugar over the top, and enjoy.

BANANAS FOSTER

INGREDIENTS

1 cup unsalted butter

1 cup packed light brown sugar

6 bananas, halved lengthwise

½ cup dark rum

½ cup heavy cream

Vanilla ice cream, for serving

Cinnamon, for garnish

DIRECTIONS

1   Place a large cast-iron skillet over medium-high heat and add the butter and brown sugar. Once the butter and sugar are melted, add the bananas to the pan and cook until they start to caramelize, about 3 minutes. Shake the pan and spoon some of the sauce over the bananas as they cook.

2   Remove the pan from heat and add the rum. Using a long match or wand lighter, carefully light the rum on fire. Place the pan back over the heat and shake the pan until the flames go out. Add the cream and stir to incorporate.

3   Divide the bananas and sauce among the serving dishes. Top each portion with ice cream and cinnamon and enjoy.

YIELD: 4 SERVINGS
ACTIVE TIME: 15 MINUTES
TOTAL TIME: 40 MINUTES

PEAR & GINGER CRUMBLE

INGREDIENTS

9 tablespoons unsalted butter, chilled

4 pears

1 teaspoon grated fresh ginger

1 cup all-purpose flour

½ cup packed dark brown sugar

½ cup rolled oats

Vanilla ice cream, for serving

DIRECTIONS

1   Preheat the oven to 350°F. Place 1 tablespoon of the butter in a large cast-iron skillet and melt it over medium heat.

2   Trim the tops and bottoms from the pears, cut them into quarters, remove the cores, and cut each quarter in half lengthwise. Lay the slices in the melted butter. Sprinkle the ginger over the pears, cook until they start to brown, and remove the pan from heat.

3   Place the flour and brown sugar in a bowl and stir to combine. Cut the remaining butter into slices, add them to the bowl, and use your fingers to work the mixture until it comes together as a crumbly meal. Stir in the rolled oats and then spread the crumble on top of the pears.

4   Put the skillet in the oven and bake until the filling is bubbly and the crumble is golden brown, about 25 minutes. Remove the skillet from the oven and let the crumble cool for a few minutes before serving with ice cream.

BANANAS FOSTER, SEE PAGE 218

YIELD: 20 SUFGANIYOT
ACTIVE TIME: 45 MINUTES
TOTAL TIME: 3 HOURS

SUFGANIYOT

INGREDIENTS

3½ tablespoons unsalted butter, chopped, plus more as needed

3½ cups all-purpose flour, plus more as needed

½ teaspoon fine sea salt

¼ cup sugar

1 tablespoon instant yeast

1 egg

1¼ cups lukewarm milk (85°F)

Avocado oil, as needed

½ cup strawberry or raspberry jam

¼ cup confectioners' sugar

DIRECTIONS

1   Coat a mixing bowl with some butter and set it aside. Sift the flour into the work bowl of a stand mixer fitted with the dough hook. Add the salt, sugar, and yeast and stir to incorporate.

2   Add the egg and butter to the mixture and mix to incorporate. Gradually add the milk and work the mixture until it comes together as a soft dough, 8 to 10 minutes.

3   Form the dough into a ball and place it in the buttered mixing bowl. Cover with a linen towel and let it rise until doubled in size, about 2 hours.

4   Line two baking sheets with parchment paper. Place the dough on a flour-dusted work surface and roll it out until it is about ¾ inch thick. Cut the dough into 2-inch circles, place them on the baking sheets, and cover with a linen towel. Let them rise for another 20 minutes.

5   Add avocado oil to a cast-iron Dutch oven until it is about 2 inches deep and warm it to 325°F. Add the dough in batches of 4 and fry until golden brown, about 6 minutes, turning them over halfway through.

6   Drain the sufganiyot on a paper towel–lined plate. Fill a piping bag with the jam, and make a small slit on the top of each sufganiyah. Place the piping bag in the slit and fill until you see the filling coming back out. Sprinkle with confectioners' sugar and enjoy.

ZEPPOLE

INGREDIENTS

1½ cups all-purpose flour

1 tablespoon plus 1 teaspoon baking powder

¼ teaspoon fine sea salt

2 eggs

2 tablespoons sugar

2 cups ricotta cheese

Zest of 1 orange

1 cup milk

1 teaspoon pure vanilla extract

Canola oil, as needed

¼ cup confectioners' sugar

DIRECTIONS

1 Sift the flour, baking powder, and salt into a bowl. Set the mixture aside.

2 Place the eggs and sugar in a separate bowl and whisk to combine. Add the ricotta, whisk to incorporate, and then stir in the orange zest, milk, and vanilla.

3 Gradually incorporate the dry mixture until it comes together as a smooth batter. Place the batter in the refrigerator and chill for 1 hour.

4 Add canola oil to a cast-iron Dutch oven until it is about 2 inches deep and warm it to 350°F. Drop tablespoons of the batter into the hot oil, taking care not to crowd the pot, and fry until the zeppole are golden brown. Transfer the fried zeppole to a paper towel–lined plate and dust them with confectioners' sugar. Enjoy at room temperature.

YIELD: 1 CAKE
ACTIVE TIME: 20 MINUTES
TOTAL TIME: 1 HOUR AND 30 MINUTES

ORANGE CAKE

INGREDIENTS

¾ cup sugar

Zest of 2 oranges

½ cup unsalted butter, chopped into small pieces

3 eggs

1½ cups all-purpose flour

1 teaspoon baking powder

½ cup fresh orange juice

Confectioners' sugar, for dusting

DIRECTIONS

1   Preheat the oven to 350°F. Place a 10-inch cast-iron skillet in the oven as it warms.

2   In a large bowl, combine the sugar and orange zest, working them together so the oils from the zest permeate the sugar. Add the butter and beat until the mixture is light and fluffy. Add the eggs one at a time, stirring to combine thoroughly after each addition.

3   Combine the flour and baking powder in a separate bowl. Alternate adding the flour mixture and the orange juice to the butter-and-sugar mixture and stir until thoroughly combined.

4   Carefully remove the skillet from the oven, remembering that it will be very hot. Pour the batter into it.

5   Put the skillet in the oven and bake until the top is golden brown, the cake feels springy to the touch, and a toothpick inserted into the center comes out clean, 35 to 45 minutes. Remove the cake from the oven and let it cool.

6   Dust the cake with confectioners' sugar and enjoy.

YIELD: 1 CAKE
ACTIVE TIME: 20 MINUTES
TOTAL TIME: 2 HOURS AND 15 MINUTES

CARROT CAKE

INGREDIENTS

2 cups shredded carrots, plus more for topping

2 cups sugar

1½ cups all-purpose flour

1½ tablespoons baking soda

1 teaspoon kosher salt

1 tablespoon cinnamon

3 eggs

1¾ cups extra-virgin olive oil

2 teaspoons pure vanilla extract

½ cup walnuts, chopped (optional)

Unsalted butter, as needed

Confectioners' sugar, for dusting

DIRECTIONS

1   Preheat the oven to 350°F. Place the carrots and sugar in a mixing bowl, stir to combine, and let the mixture sit for 10 minutes.

2   Place the flour, baking soda, salt, and cinnamon in a mixing bowl and stir to combine. Place the eggs, olive oil, and vanilla in a separate mixing bowl and stir to combine. Add the wet mixture to the dry mixture and stir until it comes together as a smooth batter. Stir in the carrots and the walnuts (if desired).

3   Coat a 9-inch cast-iron skillet with butter, transfer the batter to the pan, and place the pan in the oven.

4   Bake the cake until it is golden brown and a toothpick inserted into the center comes out clean, 40 to 50 minutes.

5   Remove the cake from the oven, transfer it to a wire rack, and let it cool for 1 hour.

6   Dust the cake with confectioners' sugar, top it with additional shredded carrot, and enjoy.

SOCKERKAKA

INGREDIENTS

2 cups all-purpose flour

1¼ cups sugar

2 teaspoons baking powder

2 tablespoons cardamom

Zest of 1 large orange

½ teaspoon fine sea salt

3 large eggs

1 cup plain yogurt

½ cup whole milk

Confectioners' sugar, for dusting

DIRECTIONS

1 Preheat the oven to 350°F. Coat a 12-cup, fluted cast-iron tube pan with nonstick cooking spray. Place the flour, sugar, baking powder, cardamom, orange zest, and salt in a large bowl and whisk to combine.

2 Place the eggs, yogurt, and milk in a separate bowl and stir to combine. Add the wet mixture to the dry mixture and stir with a wooden spoon until just combined.

3 Pour the batter into the tube pan, place the pan in the oven, and bake until the cake is golden brown and a toothpick inserted into the center comes out clean, about 50 minutes.

4 Remove the cake from the oven, immediately remove the cake from the pan, and let it cool on a wire rack.

5 Dust the cake with confectioners' sugar and enjoy.

YIELD: 16 TO 24 SERVINGS

ACTIVE TIME: 20 MINUTES

TOTAL TIME: 45 MINUTES

GIANT CHOCOLATE CHIP COOKIE

INGREDIENTS

1 cup unsalted butter, softened

½ cup sugar

1 cup packed brown sugar

2 eggs

2 teaspoons pure vanilla extract

1 teaspoon baking soda

2 teaspoons hot water (120°F)

½ teaspoon fine sea salt

2½ cups all-purpose flour

2 cups chocolate chips

DIRECTIONS

1   Preheat the oven to 375°F. Place a large cast-iron skillet in the oven as it warms.

2   In a large bowl, cream the butter and sugars until the mixture is light and fluffy. Incorporate the eggs one at a time and then stir in the vanilla.

3   Dissolve the baking soda in the hot water and add the mixture to the batter. Add the salt and flour and stir until thoroughly incorporated. Add the chocolate chips and fold until they are evenly incorporated.

4   Carefully remove the skillet from the oven, keeping in mind that it will be very hot. Pour the batter into the pan and smooth the top with a rubber spatula.

5   Place the skillet in the oven and bake the cookie until it is golden brown, about 15 minutes.

6   Remove the cookie from the oven and let it cool before slicing.

METRIC CONVERSIONS

US Measurement	Approximate Metric Liquid Measurement	Approximate Metric Dry Measurement
1 teaspoon	5 ml	5 g
1 tablespoon or ½ ounce	15 ml	14 g
1 ounce or ⅛ cup	30 ml	29 g
¼ cup or 2 ounces	60 ml	57 g
⅓ cup	80 ml	76 g
½ cup or 4 ounces	120 ml	113 g
⅔ cup	160 ml	151 g
¾ cup or 6 ounces	180 ml	170 g
1 cup or 8 ounces or ½ pint	240 ml	227 g
1½ cups or 12 ounces	350 ml	340 g
2 cups or 1 pint or 16 ounces	475 ml	454 g
3 cups or 1½ pints	700 ml	680 g
4 cups or 2 pints or 1 quart	950 ml	908 g

INDEX

ABOUT CIDER MILL PRESS BOOK PUBLISHERS

Good ideas ripen with time. From seed to harvest, Cider Mill Press brings fine reading, information, and entertainment together between the covers of its creatively crafted books. Our Cider Mill bears fruit twice a year, publishing a new crop of titles each spring and fall.

"Where Good Books Are Ready for Press"

Visit us online at
cidermillpress.com

or write to us at
PO Box 454
12 Spring St.
Kennebunkport, Maine 04046